MW01145706

A HISTORY LOVER'S
GUIDE TO

LINCOLN

A HISTORY LOVER'S GUIDE TO

LINCOLN

GRETCHEN M. GARRISON

THE
History
PRESS

Published by The History Press
Charleston, SC
www.historypress.com

First published 2020

Manufactured in the United States

ISBN 9781467144452

Library of Congress Control Number: 2020932003

Notice: The information in this book is true and complete to the best of our knowledge. It is offered without guarantee on the part of the author or The History Press. The author and The History Press disclaim all liability in connection with the use of this book.

CONTENTS

PREFACE

This is a travel guide to Lincoln's history. To fully appreciate the present, knowing the contributions of the past is valuable. To complete this project, I consulted hundreds of sources. Many are listed in the back of this book, and even more are on my website, Odyssey Through Nebraska.

Reading history was not enough. To discover Lincoln, I explored. My step count soared as I walked under Lincoln and looked over Lincoln through bell tower windows. I took tours and walked down streets to connect to the past.

To be clear, this is not an exhaustive Lincoln history. Former mayor Andrew Sawyer wrote his two-volume Lincoln history in 1916. Writing about all of Lincoln's significant moments over 150 years would fill an encyclopedia set. But my hope is that because of this book, Lincoln, Nebraska, will be better understood. Please come along with me as I introduce you to my hometown.

ACKNOWLEDGEMENTS

To God, you gave me new glimpses of You throughout this project that I did not expect. Thank you for providing your strength and direction.

To my Kyle, God knew that you would be for me everything I didn't know I needed. I love you! And to our kids, Gabriel, Zeke, Kaylee and Isaac, only all of you know the price of this project. Thanks for loving me even though I had to pick the computer sometimes. Thank you for keeping it real and for caring more about what I am making for supper than about the fact that my job sometimes involves signing autographs. Love to you and to the rest of my amazing family as well.

To Kyle, all four grandparents, Sheila, Becky, Sarah and Suzy, thanks for helping me with kid logistics all while encouraging me to keep writing. What a blessing to have such a strong support system!

To Brenna, thank you for being my cheerleader, going on photo adventures and then helping me pick the best shots. Grateful for you! Thank you also to Jonica for always caring enough to ask how I am really doing. Thank you to Tonya for the walks of wisdom. And thank you to Roberta for encouraging me to keep going.

Community is everything, and I am so thankful for those I get to live life with: Upper Room, C.E.N.T.E.R, #LNK Blog Love, LCS '92 girls, Lincoln Eagles, Lancaster Learning Link, and Girlie Gourmands.

To Mr. Rex: Not only did you teach me how to research, write and edit well, you also helped me to enjoy the process. To you and all of my teachers, thank you!

To Ben Gibson at The History Press, from our first phone conversation, I knew that I was going to enjoy working with you. Your enthusiasm and assistance with this project went far above and beyond your job description. Thank you.

To Hayley, thank you for your work proofreading and editing my many words. Most of all, thank you for asking me to clarify many incomplete thoughts that would not have made sense to anyone but me.

To Diane, for pulling hundreds of sources for me and for making the Heritage Room such a pleasant place to research. I could not have written this book without your help.

To Ed Zimmer and Jim McKee, thank you for capturing Lincoln's history so well. Almost everybody I talked to about this project asked me if I had talked to both of you gentlemen. Thank you for graciously answering my random potpourri of questions.

To all of the Lincoln locals who made this project possible, thank you for sharing your expertise with me. This book is more than it could have been because of you. Your names are individually acknowledged in the back and even more are listed on my website, as I had to tell more about my various adventures. You all brought Lincoln to life.

In September 1999, the author and her family celebrated at Billy's Restaurant in Lincoln. *Left to right*: R.B. and Florence Michels, Roylene and Dale Michels, DeLoris and Keith Gustafson and Gretchen Michels and her then fiancée, Kyle Garrison. *Author's collection.*

INTRODUCTION

Lancaster became Nebraska's capital city because of salt. The saltiness of Omaha's earliest characters and territorial legislators resulted in fist fights and a complete elimination of the criminal code. Compromises seemed impossible. Requiring slavery sympathizers (also known as South Platters) to rename the capital Lincoln mattered not. As this 1854 territory became Nebraska the state in 1867, a fresh start was needed.

The State Capitol Commission was formed. Governor Butler, state auditor Gillespie and secretary of state Kennard would pick the capital. Mosquitoes eliminated Ashland. Nebraska's very first batch of ice cream may or may not have involved salt, but the commission did determine that the sweet treat made by the Yankee Hill ladies constituted a bribe.

The salt flats industry on Lancaster's edge seemed promising. But some critical plots of land were already owned. Jacob Dawson, John Giles and Luke Lavendar were offered compensation for those properties. Dawson and Giles agreed. Lavendar demanded $1,000 extra. Somehow, someone paid. Only Lavendar's former cabin site at Fourteenth and O Streets is recognized with a plaque. In the sweltering attic of John Donovan's house, after two different attempts, the commissioners unanimously voted "yes." Lancaster was no more, and Lincoln was Nebraska's capital.

Selling lots to expand a village of thirty people was daunting. But rain did not keep away crowds on September 17, 1867. The band kept the atmosphere festive. Though it was estimated at forty dollars, the first lot sold for only a quarter. While the commissioners were there, they did not

This aerial view of Nebraska's capitol was given to the author's grandparents from a family photographer friend and hung on their living room wall. *Author's collection.*

bid. Hardly any money was made that day. Without their participation, no one else would take a risk.

After another desperate meeting at Donovan's house, they determined the capital was worth fighting for. These men would help the process. Bids the following days ranged from $40 to $150 per lot.

Lancaster's salt flats potential elevated the village to capital status. Drawing is from a historical photograph and was completed by Zechariah Garrison. *Used with permission.*

Omaha leaders accused the commissioners of filing bonds incorrectly. Lincoln knew that if land profits were sent to the territorial capital, bills would go unpaid. Ultimately, Governor Butler would be impeached over some of the early financial dealings.

THE CAPITOL

The new Capitol of Nebraska represents the most vivid and original conception ever thought out in the field of American Art.
—The 1926 Nebraska State Capitol Commission,
The Nebraska Capitol

First on the agenda was a capitol building. All Omaha architects refused the project, so the committee looked to Chicago. John Morris's plan was the only one, though he did forget a few crucial details, such as windows for certain offices, the platform for the supreme court bench and sewers. The job was rushed. Governor Butler felt that unless there was a building by the first legislative session, the capital city would be no more.

Materials were hard to find. Antelope Creek rock was too soft. Poor-quality rock kept them looking. Capitol construction was completed at double the expected price. Under the cover of night and a blizzard, men were hired to bring the state papers from Omaha.

Few pictures exist of the first building. In a short time, the local limestone started melting in the rain. To prevent building collapse, Governor Butler ordered the legislature to stop clapping or stomping during proceedings.

For the second capitol, Lincoln tried another Chicago architect. William Wilcox helped rebuild after the great fire. By constructing around the old capitol, his design saved money. Little was salvaged aside from the ball dome—now displayed at the Nebraska History Museum.

Wilcox's design reflected Federal styles. By its 1888 completion, the building was paid for. Again, settling caused plaster to crack and windows to break. Worried about another capitol collapse, discussions began about a third building.

This time, Omaha architect Thomas Kimball designed a competition. In 1920, architects submitted plans to a jury. This was the first double-blind competition. No names were put on plans, and the jury was unidentified. Four Nebraskans competed, including Ellery Davis. Six national firms also wanted the design job. Bertram Grosvenor Goodhue, the chosen architect, felt the anonymity let him experiment. His tower idea was revolutionary, but he needed help to pull it off.

Goodhue involved fellow New Yorkers. Hildreth Meiere designed most of the mural mosaics. Augustus Vincent Tack painted the governor's suite. Lee Lawrie's sculptures included the sower atop the capitol. The inscription reads, "Honour to pioneers who broke the sods that men might come to live," by H.B. Alexander.

Hartley Burr Alexander rescued the capitol. The commission appointed Alexander, Indian mythology expert, researcher and university philosophy professor, to look over plans. He identified themes that were inconsistent with Nebraska. Soon, Alexander was commissioned to script out the capitol's symbolism and design plan.

Additional locals assisted in carving and painting the capitol. Ervin Goeller is known for the *Coming of the Pioneers* stone carving atop the north of the capitol. In the carving, Buffalo Bill is guiding the pioneer family to a new life in Nebraska. As a German immigrant, Goeller arrived in Lincoln in 1924 and worked for the Forsburger Stone Company.

By using muted colors, Elizabeth Dolan's *Spirit of the Prairies* captures the wistfulness of the pioneer mother and perfectly complements the abundance of St. Genevieve-Rose Missouri marble found in the Capitol Law Library. *Photo by the author.*

While this second Nebraska State Insane Asylum main building is no longer standing, other historic buildings are still on campus. *Postcard from author's collection.*

Keats Lorenz's capitol carvings include the Native American "tree of life" doors that open to the East Legislative Chamber. Lorenz had moved to Lincoln to teach woodworking at Whittier School. Soon, his work was in demand.

Two important events impacted construction of the capitol. First, Goodhue's untimely death meant his associate, Harry Cunningham, took over. Cunningham stayed in town and later started the University College of Architecture. Second, the Great Depression arrived. The state of Nebraska's "pay as you go" meant no more art.

After completing Morrill Hall murals, Elizabeth Dolan discovered that painting private murals paid money. Lincoln became her home. The thought of not having art at the capitol saddened her. For the cost of her supplies, Dolan was willing to paint. Her artwork would go in the library.

In Alexander's master plan, his law library artistic vision included maps of major continents, as well as key religious and political figures. Murals were to examine the philosophy and administration of justice. Dolan's *Spirit of the Prairie* simplified that plan. While nobility of character is significant, at heart, life on the plains was about longing for a better life.

Ernst Herminghaus was given two months to implement capitol landscaping. He wanted the landscape selections to be backgrounds for the capitol building's beauty. Herminghaus went on to design other notable neighborhoods.

LINCOLN REGIONAL CENTER

801 West Prospector Place

Less than a year after the Lunatic Asylum opened, three patients were killed as a result of a kerosene lamp fire on April 4, 1871. When the hospital was rebuilt, limestone was used instead. In Nebraska's early days, conditions were challenging. For some, isolation coupled with the prairie wind was enough to drive them to despair. Yet little was known about causes of mental illness.

Treatments were limited compared to modern medicine. Straitjackets were used. Admittance was not straightforward. From the superintendent's early reports, one was admitted for a manic disorder and one due to lack of friends. For the first century, overcrowding was common.

At first, some dropped off their loved ones and never returned. So, some initial gravestones contained only numbers instead of names. With some community effort, today a map provides burial information. This allows closure and healing.

This hospital was once a self-sustaining community, raising both crops and animals. All clothing was made in the hospital. Due to travel limitations, the doctors and staff lived on the top floor. They were committed to the project of helping others heal. Although early treatment was extreme at times, the staff was often simply trying to keep themselves and their patients safe.

Sewing circles kept hands busy, as did cleaning and gardening. Over time, social workers, dentists and even beauticians became part of the staff. The hospital began playing music, and art therapy programs were started along with the Wagon Wheel, a carpentry shop.

Changes in the center's name demonstrate mental health transitions. Until 1901, patients came to the State Asylum, and then it changed to the Nebraska Hospital for the Insane. From 1919 to 1969, patients came to the Lincoln State Hospital. Today, the Lincoln Regional Center is a part of the state psychiatric hospital systems.

President Kennedy's Community Mental Health Act of 1963 changed mental health institutions. Instead of funding large institutions, resources were for local treatment programs. Numbers of the institutionalized began to drastically decline. Better medicines allowed the troubled to live safely in the community.

The Lincoln Regional Center is a viable option when helping with trauma recovery. Other counseling and programs are tried first. The center's mission is to help others rebuild their lives. Whenever someone is in danger of hurting themselves or others, the Lincoln Regional Center helps keep them and our Nebraska communities safe.

For those who come, hope is visible. An official state arboretum is maintained. The beautiful park-like campus is open to the public and endorses the healing power of nature.

THE PENITENTIARY

4201 South Fourteenth Street

Local residents gave away their land to ensure Lincoln was the capital. The prison property was in a flood plain at a distance from the city. Isolation helped in case of a riot or prison break. State land sales funded construction.

A small brick building housed thirty-seven prisoners. Once, when the key was left in the lock, a prison break almost occurred. After a larger prison was completed, that original building lasted for a while as a stable, a shop and storage.

Early convicts constructed their own prison. After quarrying and cutting the Roca stone, they hauled the material back. Due to their skill and good building supervision, their structure lasted a century before it was replaced in 1982.

On the hill southwest of the prison is a reminder of isolation and abandonment. Until 1958, Grasshopper Hill was the burial place for almost 150 unclaimed prisoners, including four women. Today, a local group remembers the forgotten with an annual service.

Ida Mae Lewis was an unexpected prison reform advocate. This mother of seven served as a Salvation Army member. At the time, prisoners were still wearing stripes and chains and suffering under corporal punishment. Demanding dignity for all, she said she "prayed them all off." Her efforts changed prisons in Nebraska and across the United States. For fifty-five years, she volunteered at the prison.

Streetcars once traveled to the penitentiary. Patrons could ride out to the country prison for ten cents. Community members attended Sunday services.

During a March 1912 blizzard, there was a prison break. By the end of the night, three men were dead and three more had fled. The Lincoln community was alarmed. Rumors spread that possibly a dozen men were killed, with two hundred on the loose. Citizens armed themselves, and some even deputized. Law enforcement swarmed. Less than a week later, the men were tracked down. During a shootout, two convicts were killed along with their hostage. The third went back to prison for thirty more years. Because an innocent man died, some wanted the lawmen tried for manslaughter. *The Last Posse* tells more about that week, including why some men wanted to dynamite the governor's mansion.

Deputy Sheriff Eikenbary wanted to remember his part in the posse. Rather than commissioning an artist, every time artist C.A. Dobson was jailed for drunkenness, he was given paints, brushes and a canvas. Eikenbary recalled the details. Dobson's painting, *The Chase*, was displayed on a prison wall until the building was remodeled.

In 1955, several prison buildings were burned by rioters. Citizens barricaded themselves indoors, convinced that prisoners would break out. That incident pales in comparison to Charles Starkweather's five-day murder spree. City streets were silent, and door knocks went unanswered. Less than a year after his capture, he died by the death penalty. Bruce Springsteen's song "Nebraska" tells his story.

LANCASTER COUNTY SHERIFFS

Nebraska Territory had limited law enforcement. In October 1861, sheriffs were on the ballot. The first sheriff was not called to duty. The second sheriff fled with his family after threats of Indian attacks. During the first twenty years, nine sheriffs served the county.

Flagpoles caused a problem in town. Republicans accused Democrats of vandalizing their one-hundred-foot flagpole because the Democrats' fifty-five-foot pole remained standing. Anger abounded. At the front of the saloon courtroom, gallows were constructed out of that pole. A stage driver named Pool was put on trial. So many men packed the room that the floor collapsed. Because there was not enough evidence to convict, Pool was set free and wisely stayed home for a while.

In April 1887, the mayor and entire city council were arrested. Supported by the council, the mayor had terminated the police judge for accepting bribes from saloons. Since that judge felt his rights were violated, he appealed his firing. The federal circuit judge demanded the Lincoln leaders go to Omaha court. During the trial, each was fined a large amount and then sent to jail until money was collected.

At first, the men were jailed with notorious Omaha convicts. Then they were confined in a spacious deputy apartment. Over the course of six days, notable politicians visited. The men were kept comfortable with food, beverages, chewing tobacco and flowers. Free telegraph service was even provided.

To get the men out of jail, their attorney got a temporary pardon from the U.S. attorney general. After arriving back in Lincoln via train, a band led the way as they paraded across town. Months later, the Supreme Court overruled the lower court's decision.

Early crimes involved train robberies and sometimes vigilante justice. Once, a lawman was taking a man into custody. Crowds chanted for justice but wouldn't wait for it to come. They overpowered the sheriff and then lynched the man before he could be tried.

Not until 1961 was there a female deputy. Her main responsibilities involved running the radio, helping women prisoners and performing legal actions, including taking statements.

Merle C. Karnopp was sheriff for thirty-six years. At many station Christmas parties that his family hosted, he gave the children silver dollars. Sheriff Packet was appointed but resigned after a day. Retired district court judge Samuel Van Pelt served several months until the next election, and then Terry Wagner took over. This Lincoln High graduate has been serving his community for many years.

LINCOLN POLICE DEPARTMENT

Early citizens were concerned about newcomers lacking morals. In 1870, they organized the police force. One man patrolled while two others were night watchmen. The first marshal (police chief) was also street commissioner, fire warden and board of health member. The first court case involved drunk and disorderly conduct.

Communicating with the station was impossible, yet men patrolled alone. Perhaps this is why one early police chief required officers to be at least six feet tall. Around 1894, police matrons joined the force to help women and families.

Besides being moral and civil, early police officers could not gossip or sleep on the job. Lincoln laws have also changed. In 1889, it was stated that "no person shall ride or drive any horse or other animal in the City of Lincoln with greater speed than at the rate of six miles per hour." On Sundays, the rules were stricter. Many activities were outlawed, including ten pins, fishing, beating drums and playing loud instruments unless there was a

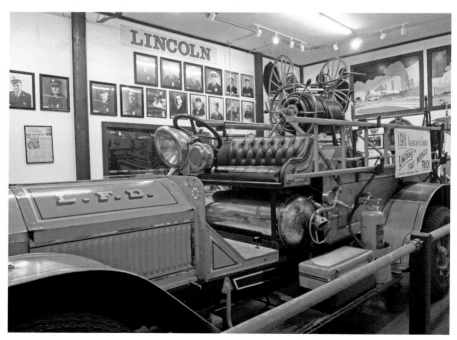

At the center of the Lincoln Fire Station Museum is the 1911 American LaFrance. This was the first motorized truck used in Lincoln and is the only one in the United States that is still operational today. *Photo by the author.*

funeral. Public amusements, including operas and theaters, were outlawed too. Only free, sacred concerts were permissible.

Through the years, the police force has dealt with many tragedies, but perhaps one lady expected too much. She sent a note to the police department to tell all bartenders that they were not allowed to serve intoxicating drinks to her husband.

In the early 1920s, street crimes against businesses were on the rise. This started the shotgun squad. One drove the motorcycle, and the other sat in a sidecar with a shotgun in his lap—ready to prevent crime. Three such squads served the community.

Over time, communication improved. The advent of the two-way radio was important. Call boxes helped officers talk to headquarters and were in use until 1976. Technology can save the day.

LINCOLN FIRE AND RESCUE

Volunteers made early fire protection possible. The volunteers were often organized out of livery stables, and horses provided transportation. Several companies came together in 1872. Between forty and fifty men were prepared to fight fires. They had one steamer, two hose carts and enough buckets to form a brigade. When the bell sounded, the gates opened. As trained, horses proceeded to their positions. Men secured the harnesses, leapt onto the rigs and sped toward fires. The whole process took less than thirty seconds.

By 1877, there were two sections of the fire and rescue. In 1879, the teams responded to seventeen alarms and saved $90,000 worth of property. By 1885, one full-time crew joined the volunteers. All were paid the following year. Stations and manpower continued to be added. Twenty-one horses were a part of the force in 1910. Over the next decade, motorized carts replaced them. In 1910, twenty-one horses were on the force. In 1919, Buck, the last remaining horse, was sold to a farmer.

Over time, additional stations were built across the city. Lincoln played a part in developing the 911 system. Lincoln Fire and Rescue station one is found at the former Q Street/Bryant School location. At this Eighteenth and Q location, they welcome visitors during business hours. Bells, badges, equipment and photographs tell of Lincoln's fire protection. If firefighters aren't out on a call, they provide the tours.

DEFINING LINCOLN

Lincoln, Nebraska, has received many nicknames: "Athens of the West" and "Harvard of the Plains," "Holy City" and "Capital of the Bible Belt," "Retail Capital of the Midlands" and "Hartford of the West." Through the following chapters, the meaning behind these monikers will make sense.

While not necessarily to scale, this late 1800s perspective map provides a glimpse into Lincoln's size and structure about twenty years after its settlement. *Library of Congress.*

1

DOWNTOWN

Establishing government buildings helped Lincoln confirm its capital city status. The U.S. Department of the Treasury provided architects for federally funded projects. For the new town of Lincoln, requesting building money was daunting.

OLD CITY HALL
916 O Street

Lincoln gave up its busy market square and ended up with the third-most-imposing post office west of the Mississippi River. The legislature approved the sale. For one dollar, the U.S. government owned Lincoln's best piece of property. The two prominent architects' (Mullet then Potter) design was double the intended size. Congress approved a $200,000 building for Lincoln's seven thousand residents. The four-story building included Lincoln's first elevator made out of caged ironwork.

For the next twenty-five years, many important legal transactions were conducted here. The land office administered claims for five million acres of farmland in southeast Nebraska. Keeping Lincoln connected was the post office's prominent position. In 1904, construction started on a new federal building. For city use only, the half block and building were sold back to Lincoln for $50,000. Until 1969, city hall was here. This restored building now holds city offices.

Lincoln's first two federal buildings are next door to each other. *Photo by the author.*

OLD FEDERAL BUILDING (GRAND MANSE)
129 North 10th Street

Of the hundreds of buildings that federal architect James Taylor Knox designed 113 are already on the historic registry. This federal building featured ionic columns and striking vertical windows. Due to the solid initial design, the 1915 and 1941 additions are seamless.

In the third-floor courtroom, many important decisions were handed down. One of the most crucial decisions happened right before the new 1976 federal building was completed. Judge Urbom handled the Wounded Knee trials. This complicated case dealt with occupation rights and tribal governments. The Native Americans involved temporarily relocated to Lincoln. The judge held campfire summaries at their Air Park area accommodations. Proceedings lasted for months. *Lincoln Journal* employees raised $110 to buy Christmas presents for the children who were with their families for the trial outcome.

Today's owners have restored much of the original grandeur. While it is no longer operational, the four-story glass tube mail drop is still visible. The polished woodwork gleams again.

COMFORT STATION (PAVILION)

Northeast 9th and O Corner

Men traveling along the Detroit-Lincoln-Denver Highway stopped at this rest area. Though it didn't have stalls, the bathroom contained a dozen toilets. A cigar shop, shoeshine stand and parcel check were available. Female travelers were directed to use city hall facilities.

From 1925 until its 1950s closure, several African American men operated the station. One was Trago T. McWilliams. This minister became an important local civil rights leader. Lincoln's Trago Park was named in honor of his family's contributions to the community.

The former federal court room, located on the Grand Manse third floor, features original oak woodwork, a sculpted plaster ceiling and leather doors. *Photo by the author.*

THE GOVERNOR'S RESIDENCES
1425 H Street

For the first two decades, Nebraska's early governors provided their own housing. Some lived in hotels, boardinghouses and private homes. In 1899, the state legislature budgeted funds for a residence. Several Lincoln citizens offered to sell their homes. Across from the capital, the Thompson House was chosen.

When he was sixteen, D.L. Thompson moved from Michigan to become a Burlington and Missouri Railroad brakeman. Over the next thirty years, he was promoted through the railroad system. As his income increased, he moved to nicer homes. Thompson asked for $25,000 for his mansion. That was the state's budgeted amount, but it only paid $21,385. With the house, the Thompsons left two grand pianos, linen and silverware.

Not long after, the Thompsons left Lincoln. His *Lincoln Star* endorsement of Teddy Roosevelt resulted in ambassador appointments to Brazil and Mexico. Although he never lived in Lincoln again, he did visit.

Nebraska governors now had an address, but the house was too cut up for large gatherings. Over time, the structure became unsafe. Afraid to light the furnace, Governor Anderson's family moved back to Havelock. At this

This expansive two-story home was built by D.L. Thompson in 1892 and became the first Nebraska Governor's Mansion in 1899. *Postcard from author's collection.*

time, $200,000 was set aside for a new residence. Other properties around Lincoln were considered. Due to capitol proximity, they would build at the same location. To provide more room for the updated house and gardens, they bought the surrounding block.

After a decade of delays, architect Selmer Solheim's chosen Georgian Revival design turned controversial. Former capitol architect Harry Cunningham criticized the "pink" brick choice. He felt that "the mansion will always look like a lost stray cat in the neighborhood of the distinguished capitol." But Nebraskans didn't seem to care. In March 1958, thirty-five thousand people visited during open houses. During Governor Nelson's term in the 1990s, the house was updated. At specific times, tours are available.

KENNARD HOUSE

1627 H Street

Once Lincoln became the capital, Governor Butler, Auditor Gillespie and Secretary of State Kennard built homes right away to encourage settlement. Omaha architects refused to help, so they hired Chicago architect John Keys

Winchell. Only Kennard's house still stands. But his hope that "a city would grow up around his house" came true.

To create Kennard's Italianate home with a cupola, stones were quarried from Antelope Creek. Walnut timbers came from nearby Garland. Two porches welcomed guests. Over time, the original house was reconfigured. In 1965, the house became the Nebraska Statehood Memorial. Updates were needed, and an 1870s Victorian reproduction was more practical than authentic restoration.

By appointment, the Nebraska Historical Society provides tours. During December, the house displays an 1880s Nebraska Victorian Christmas.

The picket fence surrounding the Kennard House, Nebraska's Statehood Memorial, is based on stakes found in the attic. *Photo by the author.*

27

FERGUSON HOUSE

700 South 16th Street

Having arrived to Nebraska in a covered wagon, William Ferguson progressed far past his humble roots. He introduced winter wheat and alfalfa to Nebraska farmers. As a grain merchant, he owned more than ninety grain elevators. Later, he owned or was a partner in the Yankee Hill Brick Company, Lincoln Traction Company, the Western Sand and Gravel Company, Beatrice Creamery (later Beatrice Foods), the Woodlawn Dairy and Capital Beach Amusement Park.

William and Myrtle's prominent house reflected their position. Due to required settling of the reinforced concrete and steel beams, construction went on from 1909 to 1911. Rather than using his Yankee Hill product, brick was imported in from Saint Louis. Innovative interior features include central vacuum, an intercom system, a rain shower and an encased wall icebox. Both gas and electric lighting are throughout the house. At a $38,000 price tag, the cost was ten times the average price of a Lincoln home.

William passed away in 1937. To protect the capitol perimeter, the state purchased the house in 1961. For the next eleven years, Myrtle stayed in the home until her death at age 103.

Today, the Nebraska Environmental Trust occupies and manages the property. Tours and private events can be scheduled. This house is also open for an annual December Holiday Open House, the same day as the Capitol Tree Lighting ceremony.

HARRIS HOUSE

1630 K Street

George Harris brought his wife and seven children to Lincoln in 1872. As the Burlington and Missouri Railroad land commissioner, he supported this new community. Intensive work and side effects from a near shipwreck drowning resulted in his death two years later. His widow, Sarah, remained in Lincoln with the kids.

Some Harris children found success in the railroad and banking industries. One daughter was a *Lincoln Courier* editor. Around 1901, the sons tore down their previous home to build their mom a new house. Today, the Harris house is a law office.

SAINT PAUL UNITED METHODIST CHURCH
1144 M Street

Circuit riding preachers spread the Methodist message in Nebraska Territory days. In 1857, the first meeting happened at a Lancaster home. Elder Young, along with several families, started an 1864 Lancaster Methodist Protestant female seminary. When it burned down less than two years later, it was not rebuilt. One author noted that this was not surprising since "of the population of Lincoln only one was a woman, and she an unlikely candidate for admission to the seminary." Elder and others stayed when Lancaster became Lincoln.

In 1868, the newly formed First Methodist Episcopal Church was already hosting a governor's reception at its Tenth and Q location. Later, that building became a school. The congregation built a stone church at the current Twelfth and M location.

Early city days required sacrifice, and funds were scarce. Reverend Hawks was paid in produce before the congregation gathered donations. When they delivered items to the pastor's house, they found him begging God for food to feed his family. They stacked the provisions and then slipped away. The man was astonished at the immediate answer to his prayers.

While the female seminary had failed, the Methodists saw value in training women. This church sent Mrs. Angie F. Newman to be the very first Methodist conference female delegate. This reformer's efforts included being state superintendent of jail, prison and flower mission work. Years later, Saint Paul's hired two female pastors to serve together.

On September 16, 1899, nearby Jacob North Printing Company was ablaze. Hoping the stone church would survive, the fire department protected other buildings first. But when interior beams caught fire, Saint Paul burned to the ground. Insurance did not cover the loss. The people persevered and paid for construction costs before the dedication ceremony. That amount would equal almost $900,000 today.

In 1901, President McKinley was assassinated. In his honor, the city purchased memorial bells. It was decided that Saint Paul's tower would provide a temporary home for them. Over a century later, the bells remain since moving them would require demolition.

Dr. Bartlett Paine, university dean of homeopathic medicine, was a member of Saint Paul's. He helped start the YMCA and invested in Miller and Paine department store. The Paine Parlor still holds church and community events.

The magnificent Christmas and Easter windows at St. Paul's United Methodist church are based on Bernhard Plockhurst paintings. The originals were probably destroyed by an Allied firebomb raid on the Nazis in Germany in 1944. *Photo by the author.*

In 1915, Billy Sunday preached to "stir up faith in Lincoln." On March 1, 1927, the first performance of the Lincoln (Little) Symphony happened in the sanctuary. Before she sang at the Lincoln Memorial to thousands of people, Marian Anderson performed at Saint Paul's in March 1938. This church provided Lincoln's first televised church services.

FIRST BAPTIST CHURCH

1340 K Street

The friendly church with the vital message.

On August 22, 1869, fourteen Baptists organized this church. Brother Conger was the determined first pastor. One Sunday morning, he woke to a flooded Antelope Creek blocking his way. Without a bridge, he put his church clothes in a tub and then waded across. He made it to preach on time.

After initial meetings in the capitol senate chamber, the congregation built a church at Eleventh and L Streets. During the second service in the building, they held Sunday school for one student and a baptismal service. In 1888, the congregation moved to Fourteenth and K when a new Gothic church was completed. By the twenty-fifth anniversary, the church had more than one thousand members.

Expanding church reach mattered. Revival services had two thousand in attendance. The result was new members and more Baptist churches. Missionaries were sent from the congregation. The Axlings shared the gospel and impacted the United States' foreign policy with Japan.

In 1964, leadership chose to build a modern building. In preparation, they uncovered the 1887 copper cornerstone. Saved newspaper articles from that cornerstone told of street troubles, law breakers and trouble overseas. Similar concerns were happening in the 1960s. At both dedications, the mayor and governor were in attendance.

Due to changes in downtown population and city organization, First Baptist's numbers have declined. But now they host three ethnic congregations: Mandarin Chinese, South Sudanese and a Myanmar Karen Church. All three were part of First Baptist's August 2019 sesquicentennial celebration.

FIRST CHRISTIAN CHURCH
430 South 16th Street

In 1868, Nebraska legislative chaplain Dungan was the preacher. First Christian Church officially started services on January 24, 1869. At first, they met in homes, the schoolhouse and the capitol. With three state lots, they built at Tenth and K. Then the church helped establish Bethany's Cotner College.

With five hundred members, the new Fourteenth and K structure was impressive. Financial woes in the 1890s resulted in foreclosure. Frustrated over failure, many members left to form another church. A few years later, they returned in a show of peace and unity. This allowed First Christian Church to start again.

On May 16, 1909, the Fourteenth and M building was dedicated. The new Kilgen pipe organ inspired choirs. The State University String Orchestra often performed.

To gain a Sunday school wing, the church built yet again at Sixteenth and K. The former St. Louis Jacoby Art stained-glass windows were moved into the north hallway. Seven windows feature biblical themes, including the parable of the sower. The two patriotic windows cost sixty dollars. One features a forty-five-star flag along with Grand Army of the Republic symbols. The other honors the work of the YWCA. More about the memorial window stories and about member Governor Poytner can be found on the church's website.

SAINT MARY'S

14th and K Streets

At first, Lincoln Catholics gathered without a building. Thomas Maloy sacrificed money to complete a building. Both the first baptism and the first wedding happened on the church's first day in mid-December 1868. The second brick church was built at Thirteenth and M with a diamond-patterned steeple. It was determined to be inadequate for a pro-cathedral.

Bishop Bonacum acquired the former First Christian building. Soon after, the building caught fire. Now the Catholics had to rebuild their cathedral. Insurance covered part of the cost. Fundraising involved chicken dinners and a state fair booth. For dedication day, six hundred tickets were handed out to adults through a lottery system. The cathedral was named Our Lady of the Immaculate Conception. Mary is the featured subject in the stained-glass window.

The 1962 church updates included a lighter paint color to blend better with the capitol. In 1965, Saint Mary's was again a parish church. Due to neighborhood changes, a new cathedral was built in southeast Lincoln.

TIFERETH PLACE APARTMENTS

344 South 18th Street

Exterior Star of David engravings indicate that this was the Jewish synagogue for forty years. In 1954, the Lincoln Community Playhouse started performing in the beautiful building. Later, George Bedient's pipe organ factory operated out of this location. Today, this church houses people.

LINDELL HOTEL
13th and M Streets

In 1867, the Townley Boardinghouse opened. State legislators were frequent guests. When the Lindell Hotel opened across the street, it made Townley the kitchen to help prevent fires. The four-story Lindell changed often. After Miller and Paine purchased the hotel in 1908, they re-carpeted and refurnished it. Less than ten years later, new owners updated again.

After owning the hotel for a dozen years, Bennett Martin sold it to Union Savings and Loan in 1965. The new owners named some rooms in honor of local celebrities, such as Willa Cather. The hotel was torn down in 1969 to make way for First National Bank's twenty-story headquarters.

NEBRASKA CLUB (NOW U.S. BANK BUILDING)
233 South 13th Street

Next door to the Lindell Hotel, the Nebraska Club started underground. In 1954, Lincoln leaders wanted to hold private gatherings. After descending multiple flights of stairs, a turn at the cockatoos signified arrival at the Intercom Club. Location: Cornhusker Hotel wine storage area.

This exclusive club featured a candlelit dining room with zebra wallpaper and plush carpet. Men played cribbage, and ladies enjoyed bridge. All could enjoy the thirty-six-inch television.

When big players came to town, this is where they socialized. Johnny Carson, Roy Rogers, Dale Evans, Robert Kennedy and many more enjoyed the exclusivity. After the bank opened next door, they moved the club to the twentieth floor. Today, membership is required to dine, but groups can rent rooms.

CORNHUSKER HOTEL
333 South 13th Street

To draw visitors to Lincoln, local businessmen formed the Lancaster Hotel Company. They bought out First Presbyterian and First Congregational to get their desired property. Explosives took down the Presbyterian bell tower, and land was cleared. The ten-story, three-hundred-room brick hotel opened in 1926.

Picture of the Cornhusker's past. The former building is between the two corn and wheat "maidens" who once lined the exterior. Today, these rows of maidens are inside on the third-floor atrium level. *Photo by Annie Peterson, courtesy of the Lincoln Marriott Cornhusker Hotel.*

From the start, the Cornhusker was mentioned often in the social pages. Diners enjoyed casual meals in the TeePee and Pow Wow rooms. Finer dining and dancing happened in the Landmark and Georgian rooms. During the Great Depression, rooms cost $2.50. Guests included presidents and political leaders.

Schimmel Properties, then the Radisson, took over management. After fifty years, the building was worn out. Rather than remodeling, the First National Bank owners decided to start over. Before the implosion, Sid Conner's company salvaged the two stone and clay maidens mounted outside the ninth floor. A ceiling hole, scaffolding, nets and hanging out the window were all involved. To take down the icon, explosives were again used on Sunday, February 21, 1982.

A year later, the new Cornhusker opened. The new café, with its beautiful John Wullbrandt garden murals, was the Terrace Grill. Now, fine dining happened in the Renaissance Room.

A decade later, the hotel expanded with the opening of Burnham Yates Conference Center. The name was in honor of David Murdock's friend who had owned Lincoln's First National Bank. At the private 1994 grand opening, Rosemary Clooney, Murdock's mother-in-law, sang several numbers. Today, important guests still stay at the Cornhusker Hotel by Marriot.

EMBASSY SUITES

1040 P Street

This property has often been a hotel since 1890. Charles Ledwith converted the top floors of his saloon/drugstore/newspaper building into the Ledwith House and then Merchants Hotel. A month's stay cost five dollars.

After the Orpheum Theater opened, two hotel floors were added. Renamed the Savoy, lodging ranged from seventy-five cents to two dollars per night. Due to potential unsavory sorts at this "actors' hotel," ladies were discouraged from staying here.

The 1913 owner renamed the hotel the Sam Lawrence. For his wife, the top floor became a lavish penthouse. The lower shops were removed, but the hotel's restaurant was noted to be the grandest restaurant west of Chicago.

In 1975, the hotel was torn down to become a parking lot. The Embassy Suites became the next hotel at this address in 1999.

FORMER CAMERON'S LUNCH COUNTER

Multiple Downtown Locations

Former fruit cart owner Don Cameron opened a downtown lunch counter. Prominent men including William Jennings Bryan met around the "square table" for pancakes and interesting conversation. Pershing and Dawes were also frequent diners. To show appreciation for that time, both later contributed money toward Cameron's retirement.

FORMER ACME CHILE PARLOR

Because of an unpaid debt, Lincoln's first Greek resident ended up serving Mexican chili for a living. Instead of money, Chris Christopulos was repaid with a recipe. Vinegar was served with the spicy chili to absorb the grease, and ice water cooled the tongue. Despite other menu options, most ordered the chili during its forty-five years of operation.

NOBLE-DAWES HOUSE
1301 H Street

Family members convinced Charles Dawes to start practicing law in Lincoln in 1886. His last four years he lived in half of photographer Henry Noble's H Street duplex. In 1895, he relocated to Chicago.

From 1925 to 1929, he was Calvin Coolidge's vice president, but this did not suit his independent personality. His three years as ambassador to Great Britain was better. At President Hoover's request, he took over the Reconstruction Finance Corporation until his Chicago Bank needed help. Being a World War I army brigadier general and finance expert helped as he assisted with European reconstruction. For those efforts, he was awarded the Nobel Peace Prize.

Since 1986, Billy's Restaurant has occupied the former Noble-Dawes House. Featuring upscale dining and fine wine, the atmosphere encourages patrons to linger longer. Dining rooms named for Dawes, Bryan and Senator Norris reflect the building's political history.

This 1910s view of Lincoln includes many iconic buildings. In the middle left is the bank that was the site of the largest U.S. robbery. *Postcard from author's collection.*

BURR BLOCK
1206 O Street

The Burr Brothers built Lincoln's first skyscraper in 1887. William Jennings Bryan opened his first Lincoln office here. Until his family moved to Lincoln, he camped on his office couch. O'Dell's Restaurant meal tickets covered his breakfast and supper, and he had apples and gingersnaps for lunch.

In 1916, new owners Mutual Insurance added two floors. The building was disassembled, raised up and put back together again. Due to altered window heights, Bryan's former office is now between floors. The interior has been modernized. Residents can still enjoy the rooftop garden.

TERMINAL BUILDING
941 O Street

At night, the lit-up Lincoln Traction sign atop this ten-story building was seen for miles. This company reorganized Lincoln Street Railway. This transportation service slowed during the Great Depression before ending in 1943. While the offices have been updated, the lobby areas are still historic.

FIRST NATIONAL BANK BUILDING
1001 O Street

First National Bank opened in 1871. As Lincoln's first federally chartered bank, it survived the 1890s national depression. Around 1900, the new eight-story building was Lincoln's tallest. The bank relocated in 1960. Today, the Lincoln building holds luxury apartments.

LINCOLN LIBERTY LIFE INSURANCE BUILDING
11th and O Streets

The "Little Building" joined Lincoln's skyline in 1908. Lincoln Liberty Life transformed the building into an Art Deco masterpiece, but little grandeur remains inside. Now Lincoln Electric System uses the space for offices.

FEDERAL TRUST BUILDING

134 South 13th Street

During the 1920s, insurance and investment companies impacted Lincoln business. Due to the Great Depression, this company did not survive. With its cornices and finials, this twelve-story 1927 building contrasts with its lower-level neighbors.

BACK TO THE BIBLE

Formerly 301 South 12th, now 6400 Cornhusker Highway

God has given believers the responsibility of spreading the Gospel to all the world, and we need to use all at our disposal to accomplish this task.
—Theodore Epp

Theodore Epp had ninety-five dollars when he arrived in Lincoln to start his Christian radio program. In May 1939, three weeks of airtime cost sixty-five dollars. Epp suggested to the radio station manager the need for programming for the heart. With far more faith than funding, Epp was allotted fifteen minutes daily.

Soon, his family joined him in Lincoln. But money only trickled in during Back to the Bible's early days. Surviving took sacrifice. After a few more steps of faith, including a brief move to Grand Island, letters started flooding in.

Because of the noticeable sign, Back to the Bible's first downtown building became a Lincoln landmark. *Courtesy Back to the Bible.*

Their ministry mattered. Harold Berry's book, *I Love to Tell the Story*, shares more about the broadcast's early days.

Besides radio and later television broadcasts, music and magazines became a part of the mission. Overseas ministry opportunities opened up. Warren Wiersbe and then Woodrow Kroll became the radio preachers. Eugene Clark was once director of music. Today, his son Bryan preaches at Back to the Bible and Lincoln Berean.

Technology changed the ministry. With fewer radio listeners, Back to the Bible downsized and refocused. With the GoTandem app, people receive daily customized scripture readings.

SKY PARK MANOR
1301 Lincoln Mall

Luxurious Living for Young Moderns.

Lincoln's first high-rise apartments were designed by Selmer Solheim. While the second floor putting green and wading part of the pool are gone, the lights, vinyl wallpaper and wall cigarette receptacles are original.

The basement hobby room became storage. But the adjacent 1960s lounge still holds gatherings. Because of Lincoln's Cold War air force base, the basement doubled as a fallout shelter complete with radio, television and perishable supplies.

Miller and Paine designed the model apartment, including Sheldon Gallery art, on loan. Residents were encouraged to rent masterpieces for their walls. Upstairs, the two penthouses designed as the architects' residences are still groovy.

Today, this size building could not be built in downtown Lincoln. To protect capitol views, the environs committee started limiting building height. Ironically, one of the first regulatory group members was Solheim.

MILLER AND PAINE
12th and O Streets

In 1879, J.E. Miller came to Lincoln to help his friend operate Winger Dry Good Company. His early duties included bookkeeper, janitor, clerk and messenger. He became sole owner until Dr. Paine invested.

Not only did Davis Design plan the Miller & Paine addition, but years later the firm also designed a skywalk path to get there. *Photo by the author.*

Their two-level corner store received an eight-story addition. Diverse services were picture hanging, hemstitching, pleating, decorating, fur coat customizing and shoe and watch repair. Their mints, café cinnamon rolls, chicken pot pies and macaroni and cheese became customer favorites.

It was the first business to add air-conditioning in 1935 and become part of Lincoln's Gateway Mall. But in 1988, Dillards took over Miller & Paine until it closed as well. The downtown building contains offices and a bank.

GOLD'S DEPARTMENT STORE

10th and O Streets

On the Gold's building, "You'll Enjoy Shopping at Lincoln's Busy Dept. Store" is still visible. William Gold arrived in Lincoln with retail experience. His Lincoln store survived downturns and a 1907 fire that caused smoke and water damage. In 1915, his son, Nathan, became vice president and later operated the company.

"The best for less and proves it every day" was guaranteed. Wares included affordable apparel, notions, furs, millinery, fabrics and even groceries. Beauty and barbershops were available. Gold's served Lincoln for many decades. When the store merged with Brandeis in 1964, many were stunned.

Besides looking out for the customers, Gold's offered employees matching saving funds. Nathan continued his father's community involvement. He elevated 4-H, youth farmers and the Nebraska State Fair. To promote business, he started the Lincoln Better Business Bureau, city planning and the Community Chest. As Urban League Founder, he participated in a 1963 White House conference on racial equality.

For his efforts, Nathan's awards are numerous. The Jewish Welfare Federation acknowledged his distinguished service. For his University of Nebraska Foundation work, he received a rare Nebraska Builder Award. In 1965, he was given a National Retail Merchants' Association gold medal. He is a Nebraska state hall of fame member.

THEATERS

Lincoln's first theater event was in 1871. *Lost in London* was performed in the capitol. Until theaters were built, shows were found around town, including at city hall. University student Willa Cather became the *Journal* drama critic. Despite her youth, her knowledge of literature and theater was evident in her columns. Many an actor cringed to see her in the audience. In her reviews, she was blunt and honest. Long narratives about the performers enabled her to tell the story.

Former Funke Opera House
Southwest Corner 12th and O Streets

Lincoln's first opera house changed names. Constructed in 1869, Hallo burned to the ground. People pledged to cover the $40,000 loss. Centennial Opera House opened in 1876. In 1883, Fred Funke purchased the opera house, closed it for five months and spent almost $100,000 to remodel it.

On the drop curtain was a painted scene of Venice, and 1,200 crimson plush seats awaited patrons. Chandeliers were suspended above all four private boxes. Tropical palm trees and brilliantly feathered birds covered the ceiling. Shakespeare's image was near the dome.

Performances were often standing room only. Many notable actors took their turn on the Lincoln stage. The crowd at *Julius Caesar* was beyond capacity. But Funke could not always match the competition. Inexpensive, silly shows at People's Theater had bigger crowds. The updated Lansing Theater hurt profits—so did a fire. By 1902, the Funke closed its doors.

Former Lansing/Oliver Theater
Thirteenth 13th and P Street

Thousands of lights illuminated this 1891 theater. Patterned after the Chicago Auditorium, the parquet dress circle, balcony and gallery featured shows, "slap bang" comedies and even wrestling matches. Updates transformed the space from heavy tones to gold then to rose and green.

Eleven elite train cars brought the *Ben Hur* cast to town, where 234 people, twelve horses and one camel shared the stage. John Philip Sousa entertained along with others. Keeping prices affordable while making a profit became challenging. The last event was in 1918.

Stuart Theater
140 North 13th Street

Here Lyric Theater once presented vaudeville. Next door, Nebraska Buick distributed cars to 501 dealers in several states. In 1929, owner Mr. Stuart's investment company closed the theater and relocated the dealership to add luxury to Lincoln.

In the theater, 1,850 patrons could watch live and moving picture performances. Gold travertine marble, 450-bulb chandeliers and air-conditioning were big draws. Apartments were above the theater. For a long time, the University Club occupied the top three floors.

Based on a Bess Streeter Aldrich book, *Cheers for Miss Bishop*'s world movie premiere occurred here. Aldrich attended the 1941 festivities. *Terms of Endearment* was also filmed in Lincoln and premiered here in 1983. By then, the theater was drastically different.

Through the years, ownership had changed, but the interior remained the same. The Dubinsky Brothers announced that their 1972 updates, including a false ceiling and wall coverings, would save energy. Despite the "Save the Stuart" campaign, the new owners modernized. Regarding the controversy, the *Journal-Star* published, "One does not have to condone the changing

Although the Rococco Theater stage may be smaller, patrons can again experience the grandeur of the former Stuart Theater. *Photo by the author.*

tastes in entertainment and architecture to appreciate that the new operators of the Stuart are good Lincolnites."

In 2000, the Stuart restoration began. With some modifications, the Rococco Theater resembles the original Stuart. Reminders of the former theater, including the painted curtain, can be seen next door at Barrymore's.

DOWNTOWN LIBRARY

14th and N Street

A library outranks any other one thing a community can do to benefit its people.
—*Andrew Carnegie*

In Lincoln's early days, men and woman had separate reading organizations. Prosper Smith's Appleton American Encyclopedias' donation started the community collection. The first reading room president was Charles Gere. Volunteer librarians offered lifetime memberships or annual dollar cards.

For funding, ladies sold pies and cakes. Early rules allowed teachers three books and patrons only one per day. Fines were two and a half cents.

In 1899, the Jacob North Printing Company caught fire. The Masonic Temple, the library's temporary home, burned too. Only the 386 checked out books survived. This was the exact number of books the library owned in the beginning. Into the flames rushed librarian Sarah Burrows to save the written catalogue for inventory purposes. Someday, a deserving Lincoln librarian may receive the Sarah Burrows award.

To start over, the library needed help. William Jennings Bryan talked to Andrew Carnegie. His wife, Mary Baird Bryan, met with Carnegie three times. He agreed to donate $77,000—one of his foundation's largest amounts. Lincoln provided the real estate, the books, the shelving and a bond for upkeep.

Branches were added, but shelves continued to overflow. Bennett Martin donated $300,000 toward a modern library in 1960. Because Lillian Helms Polley financed two more wings, the music library is in her name. A decade later, two administrative floors were added.

Governor Butler's law partner Charles Gere moved to Lincoln to start a newspaper. On September 7, 1867, the first *Nebraska Commonwealth* was

Thanks to Andrew Carnegie's generous foundation, Lincoln finally had its own library building in 1901. *Author's collection.*

printed. The second issue came two months later. The paper's name changed to *Nebraska State Journal* in 1869. Book and ledger printing were in higher demand than newsprint.

In 1887, J.C. Seacrest came to town. He sold subscriptions and walked the police beat. Failures resulted when he attempted to run his own newspapers. Gere passed away in 1904. His positive influence on Lincoln libraries, schools and universities meant they all closed the day of his funeral. Seacrest had returned to the *Journal*, so he took over the paper. Four generations of his family would operate Lincoln's primary paper. The Seacrest Foundation has invested thousands of dollars into Lincoln.

Lincoln's newspaper history could fill volumes due to closures, mergers and expansions. The *Star* became Lincoln's morning paper, and the *Journal* was the source of nightly news. In 1931, the two rivals produced the *Lincoln Sunday Journal* and *Star* together. In the 1950s, these newspapers shared presses and even staff. The official merger happened in 1995, when Lee Enterprises started operating the paper.

BOB STEPHENS AND ASSOCIATES
1000 L Street

This location was an original Lincoln lot. The title was transferred from the United States to Jacob Dawson, Lincoln's first postmaster. In 1954, the Stephens family owned the property. Several efficiencies were located upstairs. Now the building is only used for business for this longtime company that offers promotional products.

NEBRASKA TELEPHONE EXCHANGE BUILDING
130 South 13th Street

This is the only Thomas Rogers Kimball building still standing in Lincoln. Although only three stories, this sturdy fireproof structure accommodated heavy telephone equipment. At the grand opening, flower arrangements seemed to play music. Using new technology, the orchestra piped live music from the manager's house.

By 1897, Lincoln could talk to Chicago—five minutes for $5.50. Soon, Lincoln Telephone and Telegraph (LT&T) added phone service. Two lines were required for citywide phone coverage. "The Great Bell War" began as both companies tried to outdo the other. LT&T bought out Bell's local interest for $2.3 million. This was the largest check cashed in Lincoln up to that point. With more mergers, the exchange moved to Thirteenth and M Streets.

The Woods Brothers Company expanded from next door. During the 1980s, the Lincoln Exchange served some of the city's best seafood inside its French-inspired restaurant. Today, this historic location is Francie & Finch Bookstore.

WOODS BROTHERS BUILDING

132 South 13th Street

Livestock engineer and auctioneer Colonel F.M. Woods's family relocated to Lincoln from Illinois. Three of his four sons Mark, George and Frank, started companies that impacted Lincoln's industrial, livestock and real estate realms. Once the site of a log cabin, this became their second office location.

Lincoln's skyline varied as is evidenced by the buildings along Thirteenth Street. *Photo by the author.*

Rather than hire an architect, employees drew up blueprints. The front façade is modeled on New York's 1913 Morgan Guaranty Trust building. Although the 1889 business is still open, this was only the headquarters until 1939.

SCOTTISH RITE TEMPLE

322 Centennial Mall South

On George Washington's birthday in 1917, the Scottish Rite Temple was dedicated. Fifty members started the "Lincoln Lodge of Perfection" in 1889. Member Ellery Davis was lead architect. Although constructed first, the temple blends with the nearby capitol.

MASONIC TEMPLE

11th and M Streets; 1635 L Street

Lincoln Masons started meeting in 1870. Together, four groups built a temple in 1883. The 1899 city fire destroyed everything but the lower level. In 1935, the Masons constructed another downtown temple.

With columns and mahogany woodwork, the interior is striking. Elizabeth Honor Dolan designed nine symbolic murals to visualize the temple's mission. Five murals are Bible related and the other four include symbols such as Sir Galahad and the Holy Grail.

YMCA

1039 P Street

"The Great Man Factory of Lincoln" was organized in 1880. The downtown location offered a gymnasium, swimming pool and Bible classes. Next door, the Hotel Capital provided lodging.

YWCA

Formerly 1432 North Street

The Lincoln Young Women's Christian Association offered basic and job training assistance to Lincoln ladies. Services included a lunchroom, help with job searches, medicine, spiritual services, literacy and even on-site housing. Two buildings were constructed at this original location, and they now make a difference from Seventeenth and A.

FORMER SPIRELLA CORSET FACTORY
11th and M Streets

Spirella expanded its Pennsylvania corset company to Lincoln. Fifty young ladies relocated and were provided places to stay. The company hired twice as many local ladies. Picnics and weekly dances kept up camaraderie. With the war came streamlining. The Lincoln plant closed in February 1918.

LINCOLN SANITARIUM SULPHO-SALINE BATHS
301 Centennial Mall

Opened in 1893, Lincoln's first "spa" had up to eight hundred daily visitors. Turkish, Russian, Roman electric, spice and plunge baths were available. An early advertisement notes that "its massage, manicure and tonsorial departments are complete in every detail." Mineral waters promised cures from malarial poisoning to blood diseases. Two deep pools capitalized on Lincoln's saltier water. Today's Nebraska State office building does not contain such grandeur.

WOODMEN ACCIDENT LIFE/ASSURITY
1526 K Street

Since 1890, this insurance company has been protecting others' interests. In 1965, it wanted to inspire others to do the same. Lawrence Tenny Stevens modeled the "Protecting Hands" exterior wall sculpture after his own family. Local stone carver Ervin Goeller completed the carving on the Indiana limestone building front. Operating in east Lincoln, it is now called Assurity.

PERSHING AUDITORIUM

226 Centennial Mall

In 1900, dollar tickets to see Polish pianist Ignanc Jan Paderewski were in demand. The first city auditorium hosted many events at Thirteenth and M. By 1928, several fires had destroyed the building.

Lincoln waited almost thirty years for another auditorium. At the site of the former McKinley School, Pershing was built as a flexible entertainment space. Ninety colors make up the 763,000-piece front building mural.

March 10, 1958, was opening night. Pershing listened to the Roger Wagner Chorale, Johnny Carson and Stecher-Horowitz duo pianists. Additional spring events included Louis Armstrong, Ice Capades, a Black Hills Pageant play, a circus and beauty pageants.

Through the years, the auditorium hosted roller skating and basketball championships along with concerts, car shows and more. Martin Luther King Jr. spoke at a church conference held at Pershing. That speech reel is displayed at the Nebraska History Museum next to the cardboard case marked "save." Due to deterioration and new Lincoln venues, Pershing closed in 2014. City officials are still determining what to do with the auditorium.

LINCOLN NATIONAL BANK

Formerly 12th and O Streets

At 10:02 a.m., five "businessmen" hopped out of the black Buick and rushed into the bank. Many thought police were on a call. Customers and tellers were ordered to lie down on the ground. No masks were used. Even bank President Selleck thought it was a joke as he commended one man on his realistic performance. No one was laughing when the robbers left with $2,775,395.12 worth of cash and bonds less than ten minutes later.

A policeman arrived mid-crime. Due to his limited firepower, he left when the lookout showed his machine gun. Many thought they saw the getaway car. But the money and criminals were long gone.

Law enforcement and concerned citizens worked to solve the case. The robbers were connected to the mob. A Nebraska sheriff, who happened to be Al Capone's brother, got involved. Although few were connected with this crime, men were arrested for general wrongdoing. *The Great Heist* tells more stories, including how some money was returned.

At this intersection are three striking artistic expressions—the Stuart building, the former NBC building and Jun Kaneko's sculpture *Ascent*. *Photo by the author.*

NBC BANK OF COMMERCE (NOW WELLS FARGO)
1248 O Street

Since 1902, National Bank of Commerce has had different names, owners and corners. In 1960, the bank was remodeled by the owner, who was the son of the original cashier. But the new bicentennial building is notorious. Before I.M. Pei designed the Louvre pyramid, his firm designed Lincoln's NBC building. Working with local Davis Design, the goal was to "make a statement through understatement."

Designs needed to be moderate and complement Stuart Theater across the street. The bank had to link Downtown to UNL. The result? A modern building that unintentionally resembles the state of Nebraska.

COMMERCIAL CLUB/LINCOLN CHAMBER OF COMMERCE
1128 Lincoln Mall

Early Lincoln businessmen united to further railroad and industry growth. For twenty-six years, the Board of Trade at Lincoln oversaw freight rates and business expansion. Chairman Charles Gere kept rates reasonable, and meetings happened at various locations.

Mergers and moves resulted in the Commercial Club. In 1913, at the site of the former Leslie House, the Eleventh and P location included first-floor retail space. The second floor was reserved for meeting rooms, dining and a ballroom. In 1920, the newly named Lincoln Chamber of Commerce organized growth projects, including Memorial Stadium, the original Cornhusker Hotel, U.S. Veterans Hospital and the Municipal airport.

In 1958, it discontinued most social aspects and moved to rent. Today, the chamber works with the Lincoln Convention and Visitors Bureau to promote Lincoln. The original ballroom is open again for event rentals as part of the Kindler Hotel

HUSKER HEADQUARTERS
1120 P Street

Behind displays of scarlet clothing is a hidden automobile elevator. Heaston Auto sold Nash trucks here. Other car dealers followed, as did a place that featured medieval swords and one that catered to university Greek pledges. Today, Nebraska gear is sold, but yesterday is another story.

WC SHINN LOFTS
126 North 16th Street

For about eighty years, lightning rod traveling salesmen brought thunder machines to demonstrate products. William Shinn operated his Shinn flat lightning protection system warehouse at this address. Atop the building is one of his original rods. More are displayed behind a glass case inside the condo's entrance.

CONSTELLATION STUDIOS
2055 O Street

Karen Kunc transformed a paint store/supply company into a place to paint. This UNL art professor is a maker of prints, paper and books. The 1910 building now shines with its customized mural.

ROCK ISLAND DEPOT
1944 O Street

The Chicago, Rock Island and Pacific Railroad line's 1893 arrival became Lincoln's last railroad connecting point. Reflecting a French influence, the small depot stands out on Main Street. When passenger service stopped in 1968, City National Bank took over.

Due to age and neglect, the walls were sandblasted. This "living restoration" was one of the first national depot repurposing projects. Union Bank still operates a branch at this remodeled location.

A rally was held at the Rock Island Depot the night the Husker football team left for the 1940 Rose Bowl. *Photo by the author.*

2

HAYMARKET

T his was Lincoln's earliest commercial area, but "Market Square" was its first designation. Today, Haymarket Landmark District is eight square blocks. Buildings just beyond these boundaries were also commercial. They are included in this chapter, along with many of the Haymarket Walking Tour booklet's forty-seven stops.

BURLINGTON NORTHERN RAILROAD DEPOT
201–225 North 7ᵗʰ Street

Greeting Lincoln's first 1870 trains was a small wooden structure near Fifth and Q Streets. A decade later, the Victorian three-story brick station was substantial and impressive. The surrounding area had more buildings. Lodging, wholesale grocers and other warehouses were built near the tracks. Today's Haymarket famers market is a nostalgic reminder of hay wagons of long ago.

The 1927 Art Deco style depot was considered striking from all angles. Sixty years later, renovations transformed the space. Lincoln Station's great hall is the former waiting area. Retail, offices and restaurants are inside. Trains arrived here until 2012. Today's smaller depot is located near Lincoln's original depot location.

The former Lincoln station and newer Hudl Headquarters, started by UNL grads, demonstrates Lincoln's progress. *Photo by the author.*

BILL HARRIS IRON HORSE PARK/CB & Q LOCOMOTIVE 710

7th and Q Streets

This newer Lincoln park celebrates train history. The stationary steam locomotive no. 710 was built in Havelock in 1901. At first, passengers rode behind this train. In 1928, to pull a variety of freight, the locomotive was rebuilt with smaller drive wheels.

In 1950, that locomotive went out of service. Five years later, it was displayed at Pioneers Park. In 1991, after restoration, the train was relocated to Lincoln Station.

Haymarket Heydays happened that summer. Both the locomotive and Iron Horse Park were dedicated. Jay Tschetter's brick sculpture, Iron Horse Legacy, was highlighted. Equipment was displayed, and activities demonstrated the importance of trains. A 1930s Zephyr, which once crossed Nebraska at one hundred miles per hour, was part of the celebration.

BEATRICE CREAMERY BUILDING
701 P Street

Near the station, Fitzgerald Block became home to Beatrice Creamery in 1898. Soon after, a fire destroyed the building. The creamery's new building started as two stories. Four years later, two more floors were added.

In 1909, the creamery moved to Seventh and L. Four years later, its headquarters moved to Chicago. Lincoln businessman William Ferguson was president for some time. With its urban location, growth continued. Beatrice Foods became an important national processor.

Cornell Supply Company, which sold plumbing and heating equipment, moved into the former Haymarket creamery. Later, an antique store, restaurant and barber operated here. Sid and Cheryl Conner, architectural antique experts, saved the deteriorated structure from being demolished and added historical elements. Today, this building's stores include Ivanna Cone, Paint Yourself Silly Pottery and Indigo Bridge Books.

Outside, visitors can sit on the *Watchful Citizen* bench. Betty Wallace, longtime Lincoln art educator and gallery owner, donated her sculpting time to create it. Others donated money toward the foundry fees.

The former Beatrice Creamery Building was one of the first restorations in Haymarket. *Photo by the author.*

WOODS BROS./BURKHOLDER PROJECT
719 P Street

This was the Woods Brothers' first office. Many real estate and agricultural transactions took place here and then work clothes were manufactured inside before it became Atlas Carpet.

Ann Burkholder had taught art for years. Although this space was rundown, Ann wanted a location where she could collaborate with other artists. Since 1987, Burkholder Studios has leased spaces for artists to both create and display their masterpieces. Hundreds of artists using various mediums have been a part of this collective.

ORIGINAL LAZLO'S BREWERY & GRILL SITE
710 P Street

When Lou and Gale Shields renovated, they brought this space back to its historic roots. This was Nebraska's only brewpub in 1991. Lazlo's restaurant features "creative comfort food over a live-hickory grill."

BENNETT HOTEL
700 P Street

Located across from the depot, the original house was turned into a hotel. John Bennett built a 1915 brick hotel. Thirty rooms were upstairs, and the ground floor had a restaurant. Later, Lazlo's owners tried an updated international restaurant concept with Jabrisco's Restaurant. After several years, they decided a Lazlos' expansion was a better idea.

CAFÉ AND SHOP
210 North 7th Street

This 1915 building started as a café. Mid-century, this building became a taxicab garage. Renovations in 1986 resulted in an antique mall until 1991, when Lazlo's transplanted an abandoned storefront from downtown Lincoln to the site at 210 North Seventh Street. The historic storefront still stands and is owned by Lazlo's but is being subleased to other operators.

LINCOLN HIDE & FUR BUILDING
728 Q Street

In 1909, Lincoln residents could have horse and cow hides transformed into coats, robes, rugs and mittens. Finer furs were created from minks, beavers, skunks and muskrats. Cold storage was offered during the summer to protect furs from heat. Taxidermy was another specialty. Today, this building hosts events.

H.P. LAU COMPANY
231 North 8th Street

Welcome to the site of the first county jail. The Lancaster treasurer lived at this location. Besides chilling dairy, the milk barn confinement helped citizens cool off.

H.P. Lau started out with a box of lemons. Later, at his downtown Lincoln grocery, popular items sold were fruit, oysters and soda water. After becoming familiar with various brands, Lau decided to start his own wholesale company, which included a coffee roaster. In 1898, it was operating out of the creamery building when a fire happened. That event wiped out the supply and caused the owners to move forward to a bigger building. Truly a family business, the two sons were noted for their entrepreneurial abilities.

H.P. LAU COFFEE & SPICE ANNEX
TELESIS INC.
729 Q Street

At one time, railroad tracks connected to this warehouse. Milady Roaster Coffee was prepared inside. Today, the company headquarters for Lazlo's and Empyrean Brewing is in this building.

Because he was an award-winning home brewer, Lazlo's/Empyrean owners easily convinced Rich Chapin to trade his stressful stockbroker life to pursue his hobby fulltime as head brewer at Empyrean Brewing Co. Since 1990, Chapin has created thousands of beer recipes. Empyrean's seasonal beers, limited styles and year-round brews are available across Nebraska and the Midwest.

SEATON & LEA IRONWORKS BUILDING

301 North Eighth 8th Street

A Kansas foundry opened this Lincoln branch in 1881. Besides builder materials, this company offered products for factories, mills and elevators. Only in Lincoln for six years, some Haymarket storefronts have their cast-iron fronts.

This historic building was almost torn down for a parking lot. Delays saved it, and so did a new owner. Leadbelly, an American pub, started its restaurant here in 2013.

LINCOLN HUMANE SOCIETY FOUNTAIN

9th and M, now 7th and Q Streets

City horses were thirsty—at least that was the opinion of the National Humane Alliance, which sent granite fountains to U.S. cities. With its two-level design, both horses and smaller pets could drink. If humans remembered cups, they could also quench their thirst.

Having a fountain in the middle of the street became a travel hazard. With fewer horses, the piece was put into storage. In 2006, Lincoln Parks and Recreation installed the fountain in a median. During the warmer months, this location again refreshes Lincoln.

CARTER TRANSFER BUILDING

311 North 8th Street

At his home, Henry Carter kept twenty-eight horses for his mail and package transfer service. Carter changed partners and locations. At this address, the fourth floor was climate controlled to safely store pianos. Today, the top floors are apartments, and downstairs retail includes an ice cream shop.

HARDY BUILDING

335 North 8th Street

In the 1920s, this was Lincoln Hide & Fur Company's new location. Western Glass & Paint Company shared the building. Thomas Kennard had helped start this largest paint company west of Chicago. In 1927, the Hardy Furniture Company took over the warehouse. Three more floors were added.

Until the 1940s, Hardy stored furniture. Fifty years later, Lincoln Haymarket Development transformed the rundown building into apartments and retail. This building was one of the first Haymarket renovations.

MINNEAPOLIS THRESHING MACHINE COMPANY/"SAWMILL" BUILDING
801 South Street

Once a factory warehouse, the Minnesota Company had a Lincoln branch. Later, local Hoppe Lumber operated here until Central Plains Millwork took over the building. BVH Architects designed the building, complete with exposed timbers, for WRK developers. Both companies have offices inside.

INTERNATIONAL HARVESTER COMPANY OF AMERICA— DELRAY BALLROOM AND LOUNGE
817 R Street

Although the building is a century old, the interior is reminiscent of the 1940s. A transfer company was transformed into the DelRay Ballroom. Every day, ballroom lessons are available at this Big Band–style lounge.

HENKLE & JOYCE HARDWARE
800 Q Street

This is one of the oldest Haymarket buildings. For the first decade, crackers and biscuits were prepared by Jones, Douglas & Company. Later, their product went to the National Biscuit Company (Nabisco). Lincoln Hardware Company leased the building in 1905.

Five years later, Joyce & Henkle bought the property. Evidently, the company painted "Hardware" over the original sign. After some surface cleaning, "crackers" was visible again.

Today, this location includes apartments and Rabbit Hole Bakery. Next door, the Toolhouse catered to builders, and 818 Q Street is also retail and apartments.

BARRY'S BAR

235 North 9th Street

History happened here. This was Captain William Donovan's cottonwood stone cabin. Here, the capitol commissioners picked Lancaster to be the capital. Within several years, the Arlington Hotel was here. Oscar Wilde was a guest, but he was not impressed with the newer town. In later years, farmers brought cream to this location. Boilers were built here in the 1940s. Remodeling resulted in Barry's Bar, a popular Husker fans location.

HUBER BUILDING

803 Q Street

Before coming to Lincoln, Huber traction engines won all of the 1892 World's Fair contests. Lincoln was second only to Kansas City in Midwest threshing machine sales. Starting in 1941, Port Huron Machinery occupied the warehouse for forty years. Today, this location includes Nebraska products and Licorice International's headquarters.

GILLEN & BONEY CANDY FACTORY

201 North 8th Street

One of the finest confectionary concerns in the city.

Bonbons or fireworks? Either could be purchased at this early Lincoln company. Wholesale items for any celebration, including the Fourth of July, were available.

As "good candy makers," Gillen and Boney worked together to expand into neighboring states. Golden Rod Chocolates and Football Centers were two specialties candies. Thirty-five thousand pounds of candy were made daily. During World War I, the sugar shortage frustrated the public. Rations limited production, and the public blamed the sugar shortfall on the sweet companies.

World War II brought more restrictions. To increase its sugar allotment, Russell Stover bought out candy factories, including this one. This location became Russell Stover's largest factory. Nine hundred employees made one million pounds of candy per month.

In 1980, the company left Lincoln. Today, restaurants and offices occupy the candy factory. A beautiful atrium brings the sunshine inside.

STACY BROTHERS BUILDING

800 P Street

Stacy Brothers sold fruit and other specialties. This wholesale company operated for a long time before similar businesses took over. Today, the bottom floor is home to the Mill, a popular local coffee shop.

HARPHAM BROTHERS BUILDING

803 P Street

Four Harpham brothers arrived in town around 1884. Along with clothing for horses, their trade became saddles and harness hardware. Over fifty employees worked in the factory, "some of them being very efficient and skilled workmen."

Behind the original building, a horse collar factory was added in 1912. Automobile upholstery, briefcases and golf bags were available through the 1950s. Today, apartments are upstairs. From the lower level, Vincenzos has been serving Italian food for more than twenty years.

VEITH BUILDING

816 P Street

After working in his brother Henry's grocery store, Louis Veith decided to start his own. This distinct grocery store featured metal detailing ordered from a catalogue. Henry's business only survived on his own for six years. Through the years, many businesses have occupied this space.

LINCOLN FIXTURE BUILDING

826 P Street

Next door, at 824, Economy Clothing had a factory. But this taller structure distributed plumbing supplies. Both Hardy Furniture and Miller & Paine used this arched window building as a warehouse. Old Chicago's Pizza has occupied the lower level since 1996.

RIDNOUR BUILDING
809 P Street

Ridnour offered furnishing and notions at wholesale prices. This company also created clothes for the working man. A variety of shops are open here, including a Russian specialty store.

LINCOLN DRUG COMPANY BUILDING (NOW APOTHECARY)
140 North 8th Street

In the days before big medicine, a local laboratory was required to mix pharmaceuticals. This company sold school and soda fountain supplies, as well as cigars and tobacco. The company's own brand, Eldeco, included farm and household supplies. Today, specialty shops and offices are on the lower floors. Upstairs, the lofts are event spaces.

SALVATION ARMY
749 P Street

A favorite of traveling theater groups, the Tremont House offered sixty-two hotel rooms. Graingers remodeled the building into its 1904 headquarters. Sixty-two years later, the Salvation Army decided not to remodel but to start over.

The Salvation Army started in Lincoln in the fall of 1888. This group was committed to community involvement. With its religious focus, it made a difference in the lives of children and the community. The 1966 building kept the same footprint, so it blends into the Haymarket neighborhood. When the Salvation Army moved to Twenty-Seventh and Holdrege, this building became offices.

GRAINGER BROTHERS
733–737 P Street and 105 and 151 North Eighth 8th Street

Being the sole area agents for the California Fruit Exchange must have been quite the accomplishment for the Grainger brothers. The brothers arrived in Lincoln around 1881 from England. In 1887, they started their wholesale fruit and produce house.

Ten years later, "choice family and staple groceries" were added to the shelves. During their early years, about a dozen salespeople always traveled to get product to their Nebraska and Midwest markets. For some time, the brothers also marketed their Nebria products, including Kiro Coffee. Grainger closed in the 1960s.

ARMOUR BUILDING
100 North 8th Street

Many small hotels operated here during Lincoln's earlier days. In 1911, this became a meatpacking plant for Armour. Fine materials were used in the construction of this plant.

RAYMOND BROTHERS BUILDING
801 O Street

When the Raymonds came to Lincoln in 1872, they had plans to sell groceries to the public and wholesalers. But when their several hundred dollars' worth of product sold out on the sidewalks before making it to the shelves, they decided to be only wholesalers. Other owners were glad to no longer have to drive to Omaha for supplies.

HARGREAVES BROS./SCHWARZ PAPER BUILDING
747 O Street

This was another wholesale grocer. A.E. Hargreaves came from England. At first, he sold peanuts at a stand. Fourteen years later, his company had sales of $100 million. Schwarz Paper Company took over in 1917 and operated here for almost a century before moving across town.

PEPPERBERG SEGAR FACTORY
815 O Street

As a college student, Roy Pepperberg designed his father, Julius's, new store. Pepperberg's Segar relocated from Plattsmouth. It made and sold cigars to retailers for a few decades.

The horse-drawn streetcar is from the town's early days. To get to the train, Lincoln Hotel guests walked west two blocks down the hill. *Author's collection.*

HOTEL LINCOLN

141 North 9th Street

When the owners announced plans to build another seven-story hotel, many were confused. By 1890, Lincoln already had two thousand lodging rooms, and more did not seem necessary. But this hotel was popular immediately and even needed an addition less than twenty years later. Many social and political gatherings took place here.

In 1972, Lincoln Hilton took over the property. The new hotel building included a parking garage. It was then sold to Holiday Inn. Today, the Graduate Lincoln Hotel brings 1960s flair to the capital.

HARRIS OVERPASS

On December 1, 1955, the new Harris Overpass into Lincoln opened. Despite becoming a New York securities advisor and railroad financier, John Harris remembered his Lincoln roots. While the bridge is for automobiles, the intention is to remind travelers of the rugged roads pioneers took to Lincoln.

VOIGHT MEAT MARKET AND BIRD WINDMILL BUILDING/ NOYES GALLERY

115 and 121 South 9th Street

When the former secondhand store closed, Fred Voight opened his meat market in 1888. This butcher was in operation for sixty-three years. Next door was the Bird Windmill Company. It sold Kalamazoo Windmills and supplies. Another portion of this location featured boots on the bottom and lodging on top.

Since the 1970s, art galleries have occupied these spaces. Julia Noyes opened her creative cooperative in 1993. More than 125 local artists create and exhibit their work.

PEANUT BUTTER FACTORY

301 South 9th Street

James Frederick Garvey moved to Lincoln when he was fifteen. Ten years later, he started manufacturing food and household products. After purchasing a stone mill, peanut butter became one of his products. Garvey was a founding member of the National Peanut Butter Manufacturers' Association.

After Garvey's death in 1942, George Mechling took over. In 1949, a fire started in a peanut roaster. Due to all of the oils, the flames spread quickly. This became one of the biggest Lincoln fires ever. Two trucks full of peanut butter were saved, but as the basement was filled with water, cleanup and restoration were required.

In the 1950s, Garvey Food Products included various peanut butters, oils, candies and other condiments. At one time, Garvey manufactured 250,000 pounds of peanut butter weekly. Today, this former factory offers office and retail spaces.

COLOR COURT BUILDING

825 M Street

This 1892 building is actually a part of the original city plat. Lincoln Paint and Color Company had its offices and manufacturing plant here. In 2009, the building was completely remodeled as an office building.

CURTIS, TOWLE AND PAINE

8th and M Streets

Although this was a national company, Curtis, Towle and Paine fully invested in Lincoln. This woodwork manufacturing company had easy access to the railroad. Facilities included an employees' locker room, library and club room.

To display products, a four-room apartment was constructed on-site. This was furnished with all of the options the company offered, so potential builders could see the possibilities. Today, some of the brick buildings are still standing.

LINCOLN BASEBALL

Since 2000, Haymarket Park has been home to the semiprofessional team the Lincoln Saltdogs. The field has won Best Baseball Field of the Year several times. But through the years, ball was played in many parts of town.

Fans at Lincoln's first baseball games cheered for the Tree Planters. Men paid a quarter, and ladies were free. Durfee Park at Seventeenth and Van Dorn Streets was the first location. Determining a mascot must have been challenging, since later teams were known as Ducklings, Greenbackers, Railsplitters, Tigers and Links. With the change of names came many changes of field locations, including Antelope Park.

Early teams were decent, but no Western League championships were won. Well-known players did come to Lincoln to play. One was Pitcher Ed Cicott, who was part of the Chicago Black Sox scandal.

The City of Lincoln built Sherman Field in 1947 near Second and South Streets. During the 1940s and 1950s, the Lincoln Chiefs played at this site. Crowds sitting on the wooden bleachers were treated to watching players, such as Satchel Paige, Nellie Fox and Bobby Shantz. Today, Sherman Field is used for high school and American Legion ball.

3

UNIVERSITY OF NEBRASKA–LINCOLN (UNL)

Newly formed states in the western United States, with their democratic ideals and relatively classless societies, provided the perfect environment in which this new kind of education could flourish.
—*Kay Logan-Peters*

Justin Morrill desperately wanted to go to college. Due to financial restraints, he pursued self-education. In 1854, he started his forty-four-year Congress career. This Vermont man wanted more options for others. He sponsored the 1862 Morrill Land-Grant Act. Government land sales would benefit schools with programs in agriculture, business, engineering, home economics and mechanics. Newly formed Nebraska had potential funds for its state university.

When the university started, Lincoln was surrounded by raw prairie. Streets were dirt, and the railroad had yet to arrive. Early educators had vision.

FORMER UNIVERSITY HALL

Center of the Four-Block Campus (R–T Streets and 10th–12th Streets)

For a small town, this multistory building seemed impressive when it was built. After all, University Hall had a chapel, rooms for recitation, school societies, musical performance and laboratories for storing specimens. An armory, a ladies' gathering room and a printing office were additional features. At first, Frank Billings even kept hogs in the basement.

Unfortunately, the building was poorly constructed. Before classes even started, the foundation had to be replaced. Repairs kept coming. In 1925, to save the structure, leadership removed the top two floors. In 1948, the building was torn down. Today, the original school bell is at the Wick Alumni Center garden.

ARCHITECTURE HALL

400–402 Stadium Drive

For the first fifteen years of university history, finding a book on campus was challenging. Texts were spread across multiple buildings. Faculty had keys to the libraries, but there were no set hours. When this building was built as a library in 1895, students must have been grateful. The Nebraska State Historical Society moved its ten thousand books into the first floor for a few decades. On the second floor, the university displayed its own books.

Three flights of stairs led to the art department. Due to propriety, using actual art models was not permitted at first. Some statues used to provide perspective for the artists are still found around the building. Mechanical and freehand drawing instruction happened on this floor.

Once Love Library was built, the books moved to that larger location. For a short time, this location became Navy Hall. Since 1947, this building has been known as Architecture Hall. Classrooms and offices are on the lower levels, with artist studios on the top floors. From 1985 until 1987, the building was renovated and linked to the Old Law College.

OLD LAW COLLEGE

10ᵗʰ and R Streets

One of the university's most notable professors, Roscoe Pound, was born in Lincoln. Due to his incredible memory, he was brilliant. By thirteen, he was attending the university, and he received his doctorate as a teen. He directed the Nebraska Botanical Survey. While he was dean of UNL law right after the turn of the century, he worked on forming uniform state school laws.

Pound passed the bar but never had an official law diploma. Through the years, he received two hundred worldwide honorary degrees. Students

Known as Architecture Hall, this is one of UNL's oldest buildings. *Photo by the author.*

The perched copper owl was once part of a pair before it was stolen from the top of Architecture Hall. Its new location on the Old Law Building protects it from harm. *Photo by the author.*

appreciated how he interacted with them. His innovative approach also involved analyzing representative cases. For twenty years, he was Harvard Law dean and later a law professor.

At first, prospective lawyers studied in University Hall. In 1911, the legislature appointed money for a law building. Today, the former façade is under glass.

In the spring of 1975, the law college moved to East Campus. Three years later, the Ross McCollum building was complete. Some of his petroleum fortune supported high-level education.

LOVE LIBRARY

1318 R Street

With former mayor Don Love's $850,000 donation, a new library was built. Before the books were moved, World War II started, and barracks were needed. By 1945, troops were out of the building, so books could move inside. This became the largest building on campus. With a later north addition, the campus quadrangle disappeared.

At night, Love Library on the university's main campus glows Husker red. *Photo by the author.*

TEMPLE BUILDING

1209 R Street

John D. Rockefeller's oil money was not welcome in Nebraska—at least William Jennings Bryan felt that way. But when Chancellor Benjamin Andrews asked his longtime friend to help fund a student activity building, Rockefeller was happy to help. He donated two-thirds of the money while Andrews raised the remaining $33,333. To satisfy protestors, it was built off campus.

At first, the location was to offer both social and spiritual functions. Hosting religious events at a state school bothered certain citizens. Since dances happened often, the concern over potential religious events faded away.

BESSEY HALL

1215 U Street

In 1884, Charles Bessey was recruited away from Iowa State. This hire might be UNL's most important one. His motto, "science with practice," changed the science program. Besides multiple years as chancellor and "dean of deans," he helped organize East Campus's farm programs.

In 1915, a new botany/zoology building was under construction. Bessey died suddenly that year. The new building was named Bessey Hall in his honor. In the 1980s, necessary renovations preserved this part of UNL history. Students were grateful for air-conditioning.

MEMORIAL STADIUM

1 Memorial Stadium Drive

Not the victory but the action, not the goal but the game, in the deed, the glory.
—Hartley Burr Alexander, UNL professor of philosophy
(inscription on stadium)

The 1889 Harvard-Yale football game changed Nebraska's history. After watching that game, UNL alumni Roscoe Pound determined that Nebraska needed football. Chancellor Canfield agreed. Hosting games would be a community connection.

This 1925 postcard demonstrates that the university was still on the edge of town. At this point, both Memorial Stadium and the Coliseum were completed, with Morrill Hall shown under construction. *Stephanie Grace Whitson's collection.*

First tickets cost a quarter. Early mascot names included Tree Planters, Antelopes, Rattlesnake Boys and Bugeaters. Courtesy of a sports reporter, Cornhuskers became the final selection.

A big early win was the team's defeat of the University of Notre Dame. Since Knute Rockne and the "Four Horsemen" were on Notre Dame's team at the time, it was quite the feat. Joe Putjenter designed the "Guardians of the Gate" that honors early Huskers. This door found at the end of the tunnel walk features Bob Brown, George Sauer, George Flippin, Guy Chamberlin, Sam Francis and Bob Reynolds. As Nebraska's first African American player, Flippin fought for equality.

In 1923, the university needed a new stadium. Naming it "Memorial" would honor Nebraska's World War I soldiers. Initial plans also included a World War I museum, a Veterans club and a gymnasium. But the legislature limited the budget. To finish the field, the alumni association collected donations.

Ellery Davis's father had been dean of arts and sciences. In honor of him, Davis donated his time as an architect. John Latenser, who also designed the temple building, did the same.

Most people know about the team successes under Coaches Devaney and Osborne. Earlier, from 1929 to 1936, Coach Dana Bible's Huskers won six Big Six championships.

This gate was the original entrance to the fenced campus. Chancellor Burnett convinced the Omaha Burlington Railroad to donate and deliver the twenty-four-foot-high former depot columns. But his dream of an "Avenue of a Thousand Columns" never progressed beyond the original donation. *Photo by the author.*

Today's Memorial Stadium is quite different from the original. Numerous additions and skyboxes have expanded the crowd capacity from 31,080 to more than 90,000 people. Since 1962, all of Nebraska's home football games have been sold out. Nebraska leads the nation with over 375 consecutive sellout games.

NEBRASKA COLISEUM

1350 Vine Street

Once the outdoor sporting facility was completed, the university needed a place for indoor gatherings. For fifty years, the Nebraska Coliseum hosted commencements and sporting events. Dances were popular gatherings, especially when the Glen Miller and Tommy Dorsey bands came to Lincoln. Nebraska volleyball played here until 2013. Today, students enjoy all sorts of recreation here.

For more than twenty years, Archie the Mammoth has been greeting Nebraska State Museum visitors. *Photo by the author.*

MORRILL HALL

645 North 14ᵗʰ Street

Many might consider Charles Morrill an amateur archaeologist. Erwin H. Barbour, his friend and natural history museum director, convinced him to fund many western Nebraska digs. Morrill wanted to fund buildings to store the specimens.

Despite Nebraska Hall's frequent fires, this hall initially stored the artifacts. Thomas Kimball designed a museum, but only one wing was built at first. Fireproof materials were used, but faulty wiring still resulted in the structure burning down. Some items were destroyed. Repairs were made, and the specimens stayed.

Morrill wanted a better building. He promised some funding if the construction was accelerated, and $300,000 was set aside by the legislature. Architect Ellery Davis had never planned a museum before. Dr. Barbour toured other state museums with Davis so they could study lighting and displays.

Morrill's money went toward interior decorations. Elizabeth Dolan was commissioned to paint the murals. Martha McKelvie, the former governor's wife, contributed additional art. Displays still focus on Nebraska's natural history.

MUELLER TOWER
1307 U Street

For five years, the university had missed the sound of bells. When the University Hall bell tower had to be removed for safety purposes, the campus had been strangely silent. Due to the Great Depression, the bells were put on hold. After World War II, the project was possible again.

Ralph Mueller, an 1898 alum, made his fortune in the field of electronics. He donated $90,000 toward the construction of the tower. Instead of bells, chimes would sound from finely tuned rods using a player piano concept. This appealed to Mueller—so did a towering ear of corn to house the chimes.

The university decided to hold a contest for the tower design. Upper-level architecture students were allowed to participate. George Kuska won. Although he dismissed the ear of corn idea, the row of corn surrounding the top of the tower fulfilled Mueller's design hopes.

For a long time, only limited songs could play at scheduled times. Today, 750 songs are possible. With remote accessibility, chimes are often heard across campus.

PERSHING MILITARY AND NAVAL SCIENCE BUILDING
1400 R Street

John J. Pershing taught at a country schoolhouse before attending West Point. In 1891, he started his four years as the university professor of military science and tactics. To "take a body of corn-fed yokels and turn them into fancy cadets, almost indistinguishable from West Pointers" was a big task.

One task involved leading students in drills. His expectations led to perfection. In national drill competitions, the university cadets received recognition. The group renamed itself the "Pershing Rifles" in his honor. Even after his departure from Nebraska, he sometimes checked with the group to make sure precision still mattered.

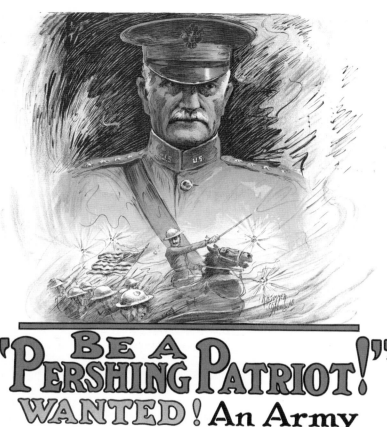

Lincoln adopted and admired its former UNL professor. During World War I, the newspaper ran "Pershing's Casualty List" to announce soldiers' sacrifices. *Library of Congress.*

When Pershing left Lincoln, he led African Americans during the Spanish-American War. This led to his "Black Jack" nickname. Later service in Asia involved cultural immersion and language learning. In 1906, he was appointed brigadier general over eight hundred soldiers.

Tragedy entered Pershing's life in 1914, when his wife and three young daughters died in a San Francisco house fire. Though devastated, he moved on. He brought his son back to Lincoln to live with his sister and then continued in the military.

Soon, he was chasing down Pancho Villa. In 1917, he was commanding all American soldiers of the European land forces under President Wilson. After World War I, he was named general of the armies and became the first six-star general.

Through the years, Pershing returned to his house in Lincoln. When he died, he left a large gift to the university. In the lobby of the Pershing Military and Naval Science building, displays tell more of Pershing's story. During business hours, visitors can learn more about this notable man.

KIMBALL'S ADMINISTRATION BUILDING (NOW SHELDON ART GALLERY)

12th and R Streets

The great advantage of the university museum is the irretrievable opportunity of serving the young, before the patterns of observation and experience are structured, while there is still a kind and a degree of openness that are crowded out in later life.

—*Frank Stanton, president of CBS,*
at Sheldon Memorial Art Gallery Dedication on May 16, 1963

Lincoln's very first art exhibit happened at the post office. Around Christmas 1888, crowds lined up to see *The Wise and Foolish Virgins* by Piloty. High demand required special trains to get people to Lincoln. Folks traveled from miles around to see this work of art that is still part of the collection. The Haydon Art Club, later Nebraska Art Association, knew that Nebraska was ready for art.

Mr. and Mrs. Hall were some of the first to join the Nebraska Art Association. In their home, artwork was displayed from their world travels. Their collection added culture to the community. In 1928, they donated the pieces to the university for its collection.

At the back of the Sheldon Museum of Art is *Wind Sculpture III*, as completed by Yinka Shonibare. *Photo by the author.*

For pieces to be purchased, there was a contest. Annual exhibitions would allow available art to be exhibited for potential purchases. Today, staff, consultants and committees work together to expand the collection.

During the early years, art was around many buildings. Art instruction happened in the upper library levels. Later, the collection was moved to Morrill Hall. Finally, the university was ready to have an art museum. To help fund an art museum, the Sheldon siblings donated part of their fortune.

Noted architects submitted plans. The creator of the Glass House, Phillip Johnson, was chosen as the architect. At about sixty-seven dollars per square foot, this building is considered one of the most expensive built for its size. With the white travertine marble, bridge staircase and gold leaf ceiling panels, the museum is magnificent. In 1970, UNL opened the nation's third outdoor sculpture garden. For the Sheldon's fiftieth anniversary, everything was removed from the Great Hall walls. All who entered could admire the beauty of this museum.

UNIVERSITY SCHOOL OF MUSIC

11th and R Streets

In 1894, Willard Kimball came to Lincoln to start an independent music school. Because the university was unable to fund fine arts, this school was nearby but separate. With forty available instructors, lessons could be taken in a variety of instruments and teaching methods. Later, dramatic arts instruction was also available.

Certificates, diplomas and degrees were available. At one time, 1,400 students attended. In the 1960s, this building was torn down. The UNL Kimball Recital Hall was built at the former location and now honors this trendsetting teacher.

LIED CENTER FOR PERFORMING ARTS

301 North 12th Street

This location was popular with university students. Stopping to get pie at the Bluebird Café was a popular outing. Then Nebraska Book was located at this site for years.

Since 1933, the university wanted to have a fine arts hall. Ernst Lied, 1927 graduate, made millions investing in Vegas. To honor his parents, he donated funds toward the center in their names. For the first Lied event in 1990, *Madame Butterfly* was performed.

GEORGE W. BEADLE CENTER

1901 Vine Street

Having a designated location for genetics, biotechnology and virology is an impressive feat for the university. Because the stacks of the building look like chimneys, it reminds some of *Mary Poppins*. George W. Beadle earned bachelor's and master's degrees from UNL. For his extensive research and instruction, he received multiple awards and honorary degrees. For his genetics innovation, he won a 1958 Nobel Prize with colleague Edward Tatum.

BANCROFT SCHOOL
Formerly at 9th and T Streets and then 1420 U Street

George Bancroft wrote volumes of history. As secretary of the navy, he founded the Annapolis U.S. Naval Academy. Landlocked Nebraska renamed T Street School in his honor in 1890. When Bancroft School was rebuilt, it housed kindergarten through eighth grade until Whittier opened.

Near the university campus, Bancroft became a laboratory school. Staff members were often both Lincoln public school teachers and university professors. Students attended until 1964. After being purchased by the university, the building became Bancroft Hall. In 2000, Bancroft was torn down and replaced by the Esther Kauffman Academic Residential Center for business students.

NEBRASKA STATE HISTORICAL SOCIETY
1500 R Street

The state historical society had to wait seventy-five years for its own building. Market Square took over the society's land when Government Square moved into its space. The society took over part of the university library. John Gillespie, state auditor, was the organization's first president.

Although a four-story building was supposed to be built around 1910, the promise never materialized. When books and artifacts were moved into the capitol in 1942, legislators finally made definite plans for the society. The 1953 limestone building connects across the mall with the capitol.

WHITTIER JUNIOR HIGH
(NOW UNL PREM S. PAUL RESEARCH CENTER)
22nd and Vine Streets

Packed with wooden theater seats, the silent auditorium appears to be waiting for students to shuffle inside. Named in honor of antislavery poet John Greenleaf Whittier, this was an early Lincoln elementary school. The first building was torn down. When Lincoln was transitioning away from K-8 schools, it did not reconfigure this structure for middle school students. Instead, it started over. This 1923 building was one of the nation's first junior highs built with that purpose in mind.

Whittier continued to be a trendsetter. "Green" building techniques were used. Tonsillectomies and other minor surgeries happened in the nurse's office. This school was one of eleven in the nation to participate in a 1920s Eastman project that provided films for education.

For more than fifty years, many students passed through the halls. When the school closed, the university purchased the building and used it for storage. Enough funds were raised that the building has been converted into an impressive research facility.

CURRENT NEBRASKA INNOVATION CAMPUS
2021 Transformation Drive

The Nebraska State Fair happened in several towns before building a permanent location in Lincoln. In 1913, Agriculture Hall was built to showcase Nebraska products. Shaped like a trapezoid, its white keystones, truss systems and skylights made the building appear open to possibilities.

Tractors were becoming part of the American farm landscape. For some farmers, this was the annual getaway and rare opportunity to connect with other agriculture families. Product displays would make agriculture simpler.

During the 1920s, when the fair was not in session, post–World War I planes were rebuilt with better engines by Lincoln Standard Aircraft. These affordable planes were used by airmail pilots and barnstormers. I.O. Biffle, Charles Lindbergh's eventual flight instructor, flew both types.

When the Nebraska state fair moved to Grand Island, only the former Industrial Arts and 4-H Buildings were repurposed. *Photo by the author.*

After World War II, with a new architectural hall, this building was used for industrial arts. Technology highlighted the progress of the railroad and agricultural equipment. Nebraska's contributions to the world were center stage.

When the fair left Lincoln, many were concerned. When the university's Innovation Campus started on the property, they did not want all historic buildings torn down. Architects included the Industrial Arts building shell as a part of their design. Agricultural history continues to be made at the Food Innovation Center.

AGRICULTURAL COLLEGE
33rd–48th and Holdrege Street Area

Part of the university land grant involved setting up agricultural education. Acceptable degrees varied from chemistry to horticulture to climatology to veterinary surgery. Determining the best teaching format involved a lot of discussion. Dean Samuel Thompson wanted an experimental farm rather than a "model" one. Staff was not convinced of all procedures, and many quit.

Building pigpens on the edge of the main university campus emphasized the need for two separate campuses. The stench was strong. Requests for a change did not achieve results, so one student took drastic measures. He stole the ROTC cannon, filled it with crushed bricks and fired into the hog sheds.

The 1874 purchase of Moses Culver Farm resulted in 350 fruit trees, a barn and land to organize. Agricultural education could move forward. Once S.W. Perin arrived to become farm superintendent, the campus climate changed.

For forty-one years, Perin carted people around campus with a variety of transports, including spring wagon, buggy and Model-T Ford with "AGRC'L College" written on the side. He was in charge, and he served everyone. While the 1867 university farmhouse was stark, he and his wife and four kids welcomed additional boarders. His wife served many noon meals as well.

Scholarships were unavailable for early students. Girls did domestic work for room and board. After completing odd jobs, boys prepared meals and slept in the livestock barns. Chores awaited them in the early mornings.

Getting to East Campus was challenging. Streetcars stopped before reaching this destination. When a new line arrived in 1903, the big

Many instructional buildings are around the east campus mall. The Agricultural Engineering Building at the rear center was the focal point. *Postcard from author's collection.*

South of the main campus drive is Perin's Porch. The recreated early landmark honors the Perin family, who became hospitable east campus hosts. *Photo by the author.*

This 1899 former Nebraska Agricultural Experiment Station is the oldest building on east campus. *Photo by the author.*

celebration involved a silver spike. In 1912, Holdrege Street was paved with brick. While completing construction, prison inmates were housed here. Twenty-four years later, the street was paved. Transportation improved once buses ran between campuses.

AGRICULTURAL COMMUNICATIONS
3625 East Campus Loop

In 1899, the Agriculture Experiment Station was constructed. At first, this building had labs for specific horticulture and insect projects. At one time, there was a greenhouse. This was also the site of the first library. For commuters, a basement bicycle room was available. Today, the building houses the Information Department.

AGRICULTURAL ENGINEERING
3605 Fair Street

Once one of the finest agricultural engineering buildings in the world, this location centered the campus. Department head L.W. Chase assisted with the design. Now, this is the Chase Building.

FOOD INDUSTRY COMPLEX
1625 Arbor Road

When Varsity Dairy opened in 1917, dormitories were provided with milk. For anyone who brought their own glass, unlimited refills cost a nickel. Numerous foods have been created and tested at this location. Today, many still buy students' products from the Dairy Store. Ice cream is served, and flavors have included strawberry rhubarb, sweet corn and maple bacon.

LESTER F. LARSEN TRACTOR TEST AND POWER MUSEUM
1925 North 37th Street

Standards were not set for agricultural equipment. The Nebraska State Legislature hoped that the 1919 Tractor Law would improve consistency. To enforce the requirements, a testing laboratory was built on East Campus. All tractors sold in Nebraska must equal or exceed certain standards.

Lester F. Larsen was the lab's chief engineer for thirty-one years. To show the progress of tractor development, he started gathering antique equipment. This collection is located in the first test lab facility. Retired area farmers act as tour guides. Agricultural drawings created by the late Lincoln artist Craig Cassel are available in the gift shop.

INTERNATIONAL QUILT MUSEUM
1523 North 33rd Street

Preserving the past is the point of this museum that began in 1997, when the James family donated one thousand quilts to the university. The quilts were stored and studied, and more were added. Rotating exhibits vary in style and theme.

"NEBRASKANS OF STATURE"

Four U.S. agriculture secretaries have been from Nebraska. In honor of their national contributions, life-size bronze statues of the men are displayed on the agriculturally oriented campus. Funded by private donations, Matthew Placzek, a local Omaha artist, sculpted the statues.

J. Sterling Morton founded Arbor Day in 1872, soon after his term as state agriculture secretary ended. As the third agriculture secretary, J. Sterling Morton served under President Cleveland from 1893 to 1897. Clifford Hardin served under President Nixon from 1969 to 1971 and helped create the 1970 farm bill. As university chancellor, he transitioned the university into modern times. Mike Johanns resigned as governor to become George W. Bush's agriculture secretary. After serving for two years, he left his position to run for Congress. While he was senator, he served on the agriculture committee.

Clayton Yeutter's statue is found in the garden his family created in honor of his late wife, Jeanne. Under George H.W. Bush, Clayton Yeutter provided input for the 1990 farm bill that gave the United States better market positioning. He is the only Nebraskan to serve in three subcabinet posts and three cabinet-level positions.

4

BELMONT, UNIVERSITY PLACE, BETHANY AND HAVELOCK

Lincoln Heights stretched beyond Belmont. Above Superior Street and Hilltop Road was Grand View. On paper, these communities looked promising. Lots included trees and bushes. Hampered by Salt and Oak Creeks floods, few people came to stay. Due to Havelock's housing shortages, many buildings were moved to that neighborhood.

Near today's Fourteenth and Superior, the Episcopal church built the brick Worthington Military Academy in 1892. At fifty dollars, annual tuition was inexpensive. Despite its excellent reputation, the school never had more than forty students.

In 1898, stored powder magazines exploded in the school's basement. Thankfully, the boys and teachers were outside playing ball, so the only casualty was the building. The academy closed. For years, people picnicked nearby amid shards of stones and brick. The air force base arrival established these neighborhoods.

NEBCO

1815 Y Street

Civil Engineer George Abel started his 1908 company with his friend Charles Roberts. With his $100 in savings, he invested in a concrete mixer, two wheelbarrows and six hefty shovels. Later, Abel was the sole owner. In 1928, he started Ready Mixed Concrete. General Steel Products was the next company added. Now, NEBCO operates twenty-five companies across Nebraska. Most involve building products. Some branches include land and surety bonds.

To support local communities, the Abel Foundation started in 1946. Its first gift was toward the university foundation. Projects have included Nebraska Wesleyan Abel football stadium. Another is the kinetic *Playful Connections* turtle sculpture found near the Lincoln Children's Museum entrance.

NORTHEAST BRANCH LIBRARY
27th and Orchard Streets, 2121 North 27th Street

To check out books at the downtown library, northeast residents paid a dime for the streetcar or hiked for miles. Lincoln begged the Carnegie Foundation for help again. It agreed to donate $10,000 if Lincoln provided the land.

Berlinghof designed the building. Due to unreliable contractors, the opening was delayed until September 1909. High windows limited distractions and allowed plenty of shelving.

The library passed on the gift of books by collecting 13,500 titles to send to World War I training camps. For more than seventy years, this library served its patrons. It closed in 1982. Ten years later, Lincoln moved the building down the street. As part of Matt Talbot Kitchen, this structure still helps others.

NEIGHBORWORKS LINCOLN
2530 Q Street

Dr. Reynolds, an Early Lincoln surgeon, possibly operated a private hospital in the upstairs of his house. His 4,600-square-foot concrete block three-story 1905 home was substantial. In the 1930s, the house was subdivided into twelve units. In 2000, the house reverted back to a single-family dwelling.

Since 2014, NeighborWorks has operated here. It helps others find affordable housing. Besides financing particular repairs, it supports first-time home buyers. To qualify, potential buyers take classes and work with a counselor. Since they are more affordable, historic homes are often purchased.

UNIVERSITY PLACE

At first, the town was called Athens. Renamed University Place, this community developed around Nebraska Wesleyan. Connected to Lincoln by electric motor line, it established its own waterworks and electric lights. Shop owners have changed often, but this section has a main street feel.

Lincoln Tent and Awning
3900 Cornhusker Highway
In 1898, this company began selling custom tents and camping outfits in the Haymarket. It was purchased by the Miller family in 1971. Today, the family continues to make and rent their own tents.

Nebraska Wesleyan University
50th Street and Saint Paul Avenue
With three Methodist colleges in Nebraska, money was spread too thin. Consolidation was the answer. Forty-five acres were purchased, and then lot sales financed the process. September 22, 1887, became Nebraska Wesleyan Day. One thousand people went to the cornerstone celebration.

Students straggled into campus in the fall of 1888. Dorms were incomplete, so housing was limited. To get to their upper-floor classes, students climbed ladders. Tuition was forty-two dollars, but less than 100 students enrolled. Today, around 1,500 students attend Wesleyan.

Old Main was the campus at first. The original chapel became an early library. At the top of the first flight of stairs, the stained-glass window *Light of the World* by Holman-Hunt still inspires.

Founded in 1889, Willard Society is the nation's oldest "local" sorority. In 1890, the four women graduated. Four men graduated the following year.

The consolidation did not solve the Methodist financial challenges, but Chancellor Creighton kept the university going, as did some of the trustees later on.

Due to the blooms once covering campus land, the sunflower became the mascot. Brown and gold were Wesleyan's colors. In 1907, the mascot became the coyotes. Students raised half of the money for a new gym. The mascot changed again in 1933. Go, Plainsmen!

In 1890, football was canceled at the school. The faculty did not appreciate the fits of swearing and anger. Young men did not act like gentlemen on the

Nebraska Wesleyan's "Old Main" is the oldest Lincoln university building still used for education today. *Photo by the author.*

field. For almost twenty years, football was not tried again. When Wesleyan played Oklahoma City in 1932, Bob Gibb ran 107 yards for a world record touchdown. As a result, he was mentioned in *Ripley's Believe It or Not!*

For a time, Wesleyan Preparatory met on campus. Classes, including Latin, were focused on getting students ready for college. The Normal teacher training program was renamed for Van Fleet. This Wesleyan alum and former Puerto Rico missionary helped the school raise money.

Before he was president, John F. Kennedy spoke on campus in 1957. During the next twenty years, nine buildings were built. Wesleyan's choir was the first U.S. group to be a part of the Saint Petersburg, Russia, International Choir Festival.

First United Methodist Church
2723 North 50th Street

During the early church days, this Methodist group met in Old Main, with Chancellor Creighton as minister. Working together kept them going. When

First United Methodist has kept the University Place community connected. *Photo by the author.*

Funded by the G.A.R., the First United Methodist's dome window features Abraham Lincoln. He once said, "The Methodist Church sends more soldiers to the field and more prayers to heaven than any other church." *Photo by the author.*

the Methodist conference leaders announced a spontaneous campus visit, the church ladies scrubbed all of the buildings themselves.

Money was tight. Still, Pastor Abbott regretted selling advertising space to pay for song books. "Hark the Herald Angels Sing, Beechams' Pills Are Just the Thing" was not his intended hymnal inscription.

In 1903, the church wanted to build but could only afford a basement. For six years, the congregation met in this "hole in the ground" church. The leaking roof compelled them to raise money. Ladies' aid circles sold lunches and dinners. All rejoiced at the December 1909 dedication day for the new church.

On hot Sundays, everyone stuck to the varnished seats, so area mortuaries provided cardboard fans. Bigger issues began when World War I started. This patriotic congregation was divided between fighting and peace but kept talking through their differences.

This congregation values being part of University Place. A minister was hired to reach out to the neighborhood. This is the mission statement: "With God's grace, First United Methodist Church strives to be a growing, inclusive community of faith working together, sharing Jesus' love, and using our gifts to build and nurture a spiritual community."

University Place City Hall/Lux Center for the Arts
2601 North 48th Street

By its twenty-fifth year, University Place had a few thousand residents. Building a new city hall would organize the town departments—fire, police, electricity, water, city council and mayor. The 1914 city hall was designed by neighborhood architect John Smith. Once University Place was annexed in 1926, this building served other functions.

Nearby, the University Place Arts Center started in 1977. Ten years later, longtime Nebraska Wesleyan art professor Gladys Lux purchased the former city hall building. She wanted a permanent community art center. An artist herself, Lux started the Wesleyan art department in 1927 with a pencil sharpener and a smile. Throughout her forty years as an instructor, she continued to spread joy.

At Lux, art education happens through camps, classes and family workshops. Rotating exhibitions often feature local artists. The second-floor Lux Museum displays art masterpieces that Gladys Lux used as teaching tools.

The former University Place City Hall is now Lux Center for the Arts. *Photo by the author.*

Former Carnegie Library
2820 North 48th Street

As a town of readers, University Place needed a library. With its money troubles and limited library, Wesleyan could not help. Years passed with no library. Residents and the town Commercial Club worked together. The Carnegie Foundation's $12,500 grant allowed a better building. Again, neighborhood architect John Smith stepped up.

When the town was annexed, this became a Lincoln branch. When Anderson library opened in 1971, this location closed. Today, Branch Pattern operates an office in the stone building.

Wesleyan Hospital (Now Saint Charles Apartments)
2742 North 48th Street and 4717 Baldwin Avenue

This 1906 brick two-story included Hotel Cecil and Wesleyan Hospital. Patients preferred Dr. Coffin's private healing rooms. Nurses could attend the on-site training school. But without set schooling standards, nurses went to Lincoln for more consistent opportunities.

The hotel closed because the hospital expanded. After the nursing school closed, a boardinghouse alternated with the hospital. Then the Street Charles apartments took over. Today, the building is known as Madison Flats.

Former Citizen's State Bank/Berry Law Building
2650 North 48th Street

Citizen's State Bank stabilized University Place for many years. John Berry started his law office at this location in 1965. As a Vietnam War Bronze Star recipient, he fought for veteran rights. Several years before this writing, the firm moved out to expand. The remaining history of this long-standing building is yet to be written.

Green Plumbing
4200 North 48th Street

University Place had many fine businesses, and one remains in the area. For more than one hundred years, Green Plumbing has taken care of the heating, cooling and plumbing needs of Lincoln. Due to its history, it has many longtime clients.

White Hall
5845 Leighton Avenue

Charles White spent the last few years of the Civil War in a Confederate prison. After his release, he received a government homestead near Raymond, Nebraska. Soon, he met Olive, a teacher and daughter of Valparaiso's first settlers. In 1868, Judge Luke Lavender married them.

White's home became a meetinghouse. Circuit rider Henry Davis stayed with them. Through Davis's indirect influence, both Whites became Christian Methodists. This decision changed their lives. Along with some partners, Charles entered the mill business. During this time, he served Saunders County twice in the legislature and was a Methodist Conference delegate. Along with other Wesleyan trustees, his contributions saved Wesleyan during challenging times. His death at age fifty-two was unexpected.

At that point, Olive decided to move closer to Wesleyan. Her White Hall mansion was an early neighborhood house. Many features are still original, including the tapestry wallpaper, the green tile fireplace and the third-floor ballroom with its breathtaking capitol views.

Aside from the open front porch flanked by columns, a circle drive once welcomed visitors to White Hall, a mansion near Wesleyan. *Photo by the author.*

Due to poor health, Olive moved in 1926. The State of Nebraska purchased her property for a home for dependent children. Group homes are still nearby. The mansion is used for offices and community events.

BETHANY

Bethany Heights became a village in 1890. In the Bible, Bethany, a Jerusalem suburb, was considered an educational center. Bethany, Nebraska, was annexed by Lincoln in 1926.

Nebraska Christian University/Cotner College

A group of businessmen pooled their resources because they wanted to sell their eastern lots to a prospective college. Baptists declined the three-hundred-acre offer. The Nebraska Christian Missionary Society, though, said "yes."

Left: Cotner College's imposing five-story stone and brick building served many functions. Inside were thirty-two classrooms, seven offices, study halls and a five-hundred-seat chapel. *Author's collection.*

Below: This former bank building is one of Bethany's only remaining buildings. *Photo by the author.*

From its August 30, 1888 beginning, Nebraska Christian University had a rocky start. Only a gift of land and money from Samuel Cotner helped it continue. Renamed Cotner College, the school stabilized until the 1893 panic, when debts had to be restructured.

Enrollment reached over four hundred, but the medical college portion was sold to the university in 1916. Two years later, the Cotner College Academy opened. The academic blue and white bulldogs enjoyed acting. Both Cotner College and the academy closed during the Great Depression.

The First State Bank of Bethany
1551 North Cotner Boulevard

C.W. Fuller was president of both the Bethany grain elevator and town bank. After ten years, the bank moved to 149 North Saunders. With the 1926 annexation, the street name changed to Cotner. The bank closed during the Great Depression. Starting in 1937, this building was Bethany Branch Library until a new building opened down the street. Today, the bank is the Gratitude Café and Bakery

Bethany School
1520–1526 Cotner Boulevard

Soon after the town began, Bethany constructed a school. In 1889, younger students started to come. Later, the older students started. Carle Leavitt was among the first 1897 graduates.

The maroon and gold Bethany Bearcats were strong athletes. On the gridiron, the 1931 football team was undefeated. Under Coach Chili Armstrong, the basketball team won state three years in a row.

High schools transferred to Lincoln Northeast in 1941. For forty years, the younger grades still attended this school. Low enrollment then caused the school to close. Later, Larry Price purchased the school building. To provide affordable housing for the elderly, he converted the school into condos. Cotner Center was Lincoln's first independent living facility for seniors.

Bethany Christian Church
1645 North Cotner Boulevard

In November 1889, Nebraska Christian students and faculty gathered with Bethany residents for the first church service. They met in a dormitory. Dr.

William Aylesworth, Cotner College chancellor, became the pastor. In 1890, the congregation started meeting in the college chapel.

In 1908, the church building was completed. With 1,500 seats, the church was one of Nebraska's largest at the time. Twenty years later, fire destroyed the building. Even though the Great Depression was beginning, the congregation worked together to rebuild. Although Cotner College closed, the congregation kept meeting. For almost forty years, they presented the Easter Pageant *Cross Triumphant*, written by Cotner professor Faythe Leavitt.

Rosemont/Middle Cross Alliance
2600 North 70th Street

Havelock Christian and Missionary Alliance Church started in the 1920s. Some Havelock Methodist Church members were concerned about their congregation's interpretation of scripture. This church later changed its association and name to Rosemont Alliance Church. In 2014, Middle Cross moved, and the two congregations combined.

HAVELOCK

Albert Touzalin died of poor health before he could move to the town that he was responsible for naming. Touzalin Avenue still runs east to west on the edge of the former town of Havelock. Touzalin was vice president of the Burlington and Missouri River Railroad. Along with two railroad land agents, Touzalin formed the Lancaster Land Company. Elder Miller deeded the company 1,920 government acres.

Several communities were considered for the railroad's new repair facility location. If given three hundred acres, Superintendent George Holdrege promised to build a new $275,000 repaired facility. On June 24, 1890, Lancaster Land Company signed over the land, hoping the lots would be worth more.

With a post office, the town became official six months later. Once the large double brick railroad building was completed, forty people started work at the Havelock shops. Men came to town with their families.

Founder Albert Touzalin named Havelock in honor of his childhood hero Sir Henry Havelock. During the siege of Lucknow, India, in 1857, this hero rescued hostages. Sadly, he died days later. Havelock is remembered as a fervent Christian and a military mastermind. Around the world, eight towns and an island are named for him. *Library of Congress.*

Arrow Aircraft and Goodyear
4021 North 56th Street

Woods Brothers gave Hebb Motor Works a land grand in 1918 for its truck assembly operation. When that company wanted out, Woods purchased it. In 1926, it had production rights for an airplane. The company's seven hundred employees would make four airplanes a day. At the time, the operation produced the most airplanes of any facility in the world.

In 1943, Goodyear Tire and Rubber Company took over this location as the Havelock Distribution Center. It made self-sealing fuel tanks at this location. Later, agricultural parts were manufactured here. Through name changes, this location has remained industrial.

Lancaster Block
6201 Havelock Avenue

A grocer and furniture store combined with an undertaker. These are the first businesses in Havelock's first building. Unions and clubs met upstairs. At one time, so did the Havelock Dancing Club, which offered "good music and competent instructors" in 1913.

By 1988, the building needed to be renovated. Today, the upstairs is used as apartments. The lower spaces are still commercial, housing the Big Brothers, Big Sisters program, while next door is a designer hair salon.

The Vickeridge
6140 Havelock Avenue

From meat to hardware to shoes, this corner has sold it all. The 1890s original was replaced in 1910 with a two-story frame structure. In 1990, brick was added to provide history and authenticity. The Vickeridge has been selling women's clothing at this corner for thirty years.

Wolfe Ace Hardware
6118 Havelock Avenue

Baskets must have been quite the business. Around Lincoln, seventeen basket stores existed, including at this location. Other shops called this address home, and since 1954, this has been a family-owned hardware store.

Havelock's main street is still reminiscent of a small town. *Photo by the author.*

Lyric/Joyo Theater
6102 Havelock Avenue

This 1928 building was initially operated as the Lyric Theater. Possibly to reflect the California Mission style, the arched windows and red tile roof would connect this location with Hollywood. Across the street, the Joyo Theater had been the Havelock movie house since 1913. In 1936, Williamsen took over the Lyric and moved his Joyo Theater into this location instead.

Salvage Warehouse
6037–45 Havelock Avenue/4329–45 North Sixty-First Street

In 1903, Mintie Schmidt built a brick block building that replaced James Candy's grain and implement store. Part of the "new" two-story structure hosted the Havelock post office for more than seventy years. Other occupants included a bank that did not survive the Great Depression. Roper Mortuary also operated out of this space for a long time. Today, the upstairs is still apartments, but the downstairs now houses the Salvage Warehouse. The adjacent former Havelock Garage is also a part of the facility.

Masonic Temple
6036 Havelock Avenue
At this Masonic lodge, the group occupied the top floor with its tall, vaulted ceilings. Hecht moved his grocery store into the lower level of the brick building in 1912. On the east side, his faded Coca-Cola sign is still visible. Two newspapers operated here in the following decades. Currently, a church organization is located here.

Havelock City Hall/Jail and Fire Station
6028–6034 Havelock Avenue
When Havelock was its own town, this brick building was the center of city services. Later, the Lincoln Fire Department still used the facility. While the arched doorway is no longer accessible to vehicles, the interior feels like the former station.

Today, diners can enjoy breakfast and lunch at the Engine House Café. Black-and-white photographs line the walls that display early fire houses in southeast Nebraska. Former firefighting uniforms and equipment add charm and authenticity to this historic location.

Havelock Library
4308 North 63rd Street
Local citizens tried to talk Bertram, Carnegie's treasurer, into giving them a library. He refused to talk to private individuals. The City Library of Havelock committee formed, and they tried again. They wanted to solve the moral needs of the village. After finishing work at the railroad shop, men needed meaningful ways to spend their off-hours time.

For the library, $7,000 was donated, including $1,000 for furniture and heat. Although the Lancaster Land Company had provided the building, the space was dark and poorly ventilated. The town asked for improvement money. But the Carnegie foundation did not want to pay for rooms to be used for lectures, art and ladies' clubs. After 1971, this became Havelock Park.

Anderson Library
3635 Touzalin Avenue
In 1971, northeast Lincoln was ready for a modern library. Victor Anderson was a longtime Havelock businessman and banker. He also served as Lincoln mayor and Nebraska governor.

Havelock School
Logan Street between 61st and 62nd Streets

Drawing and music were taught in the early years of Havelock School. The distinct brick building had a large gymnasium. Starting in 1891, the crowds cheered for the purple uniformed Boilermakers. Around the time of annexation, they became the Engineers.

Like many small towns, the elementary and high schools were next door to each other. Havelock High students moved to Northeast High School in 1941, but the junior high stayed open a dozen more years. Havelock Elementary stayed open until 1979. For many years, the high school was the Goodyear Recreation Center. The elementary now holds a preschool and family center.

Ballard Park
66th Street and Kearney Avenue

History was made here on October 29, 1929. Havelock hosted the first game of night football west of the Mississippi. At the time, it was only the third football team across the United States to play under lights. This experience was short-lived.

When Lincoln annexed Havelock in 1930, night football was banned. Lincoln Public Schools did not play under lights. These lights—purchased by hardworking Havelock parents—were moved into central Lincoln to illuminate a tennis court.

Havelock United Methodist
4140 North 60th Street

Soon after the Burlington Shops began, a group started praying together. For the first three years, supply pastors came and met with them. Reverend Prescott moved from Saint Paul Methodist to Havelock. Along with the "Faithful Twelve" consistent members, he started building plans. Later, those who were part of the project gave him a signed quilt.

Lancaster Land Company donated three plots for the building at then Thirteenth and Howard. After working at the shops, the men spent the nights building the first church for $4,500. The women constructed the first wooden sidewalk. In January 1894, the building opened. The sanctuary even had stained-glass windows and carved pews. More space was needed beyond two classrooms, so the building was raised to add a basement. Debts were eliminated with Sunday school penny collections.

Hard times came. In Havelock, the railroad strike started the troubles and the bitterness. For several months during the Great Depression, the shops shut down again temporarily. Down the street, Congregational, one of Havelock's first churches, closed. The Methodist women raised funds for Bryan Hospital and other projects. For thirty-eight years, the ladies served a balanced lunch at the Nebraska State Fair. Later, due to all the heavy lifting, men would take vacation to help.

Fundraising helped the new sanctuary be ready by Christmas 1952. At the northeast corner addition, children bought bricks for a nickel and then put their names inside. When a new organ was needed, pipes were sold for six dollars each. When more room was needed for Sunday school, they bought nearby houses until the addition could be completed. Today, through change and progress, this church continues to go forward together.

Saint Patrick's Catholic Church
6111 Morrill Avenue

In 1893, the church was organized by Franciscan priests. Soon, their Gothic white frame church was built. In 1908, that first building burned down. When something rolled out of the nearby stove, recently varnished benches caught on fire. Only the sacred vessels, vestment case and a bookcase were saved.

The parish made plans to build again. In the meantime, Mass was held in the Havelock Dance Hall. Members went to the Saturday night dance and then set up for church the next day. To rebuild, the men worked on the church both before and after work. To raise money, one family held a barn dance complete with fiddler and banjo player. The haymow became the dining room. Oyster stew was served out of horse stalls. From this dance, $100, a substantial amount, was given to the church.

The school opened in 1916, but it closed in 1934 due to the Depression. In 1942, the school opened again. A blue vigil light burned with hope for the safe return of sixty-one members fighting in World War II. Numbers declined and then swelled with the reactivated air force base.

Saint Patrick's started school fundraisers to build Pius High School and to build a new elementary in 1961. One student donated her entire $100 from her savings account. The school had her turn the first shovel of dirt when the project started. In 1985, they added a new middle school, and a beautiful gym completed the facility in 1999.

The men's Shamrock Club sponsored softball teams, mixed bowling leagues, youth sports and Friday night gatherings. Bingo was once offered too. For twenty years, the church was known for its state fair booth with sandwiches, rolls and homemade pies made by the parish women.

Due to deterioration and bats in the belfry, Saint Patrick's decided to tear down the old building. First members again constructed the new church. To make the pews, church members cut down the trees, planed the wood and then built the seats. Since the church opened in 2015, the congregation has completed the woodwork and has continued to finish their building.

Mahoney Park
70th and Fremont Streets

When Mahoney Park was built, the Lincoln Parks and Recreation employees did all of the work in house. Twice as many employees meant they could build, cut and pack the roadway. They also did the rough grading of the baseball field. Gene Mahoney was once Nebraska Game and Parks director. He was known for getting donations for his programs.

5

MILITARY, AIR PARK AND CAPITOL BEACH

Flying fever hit the United States soon after the Wright brothers' historic 1903 flight. Seven years later, their plane came for a Nebraska State Fair exhibition. The pilot crashed into stables. He was fine, but the plane was wrecked. Dirigibles appeared at the fair in 1907. Even though many pilots died young, learning to fly was popular. Lincoln impacted aviation.

LINCOLN AIRPLANE AND FLYING SCHOOL
24th and O Streets

Lincoln Auto School first started seven blocks east of this location. This mechanic trade school lasted eight years before tractors were added to the title. Houses were torn down to build a two-story, sixty-thousand-square-foot building, complete with a basement, near Twenty-Fourth and O Streets.

The new building was a welcome site to A.G. Hebb. He had already found success manufacturing trucks in Havelock. By leasing part of the warehouse, he could start the Nebraska Aircraft/Lincoln Standard Aircraft Company. The school operated out of the rest of the building and added aircraft mechanics to its curriculum. In 1921, Ray Page joined the staff and then purchased Nebraska Aircraft the following year.

LINDBERGH

For months, I had been assembling flying-school catalogues. One of them offered training at Lincoln, Nebraska for five hundred dollars. It was a price my father and mother could afford, and to me the name "Nebraska" was full of romance.

—*Charles Lindbergh,* An Autobiography of Values

Rarely is someone grateful to fail college, but if Charles Lindbergh had become an engineer like he intended, he might not have changed the world. Aviation became his inspiration.

Lindbergh may not have gotten the cockpit hours he paid for at the Nebraska Standard Flying School. His instructor's enthusiasm for flying had faltered after a friend died in a crash. One fact is certain, though: Lindbergh left town knowing more than how to pilot a plane.

Part of the instruction involved becoming an airplane mechanic. Lindbergh taught himself to overcome fears as he learned to wing walk and parachute jump. Because of his time in Lincoln, Lindbergh was able to move on to more aviation experiences.

NEBRASKA NATIONAL GUARD IN LINCOLN
Northwest 25th Street

After the Civil War, the nation was tired of fighting. Since Nebraska was formed less than five years following the cease fire, this impacted the state. First, many Nebraska towns and counties were named for soldiers. Second, many moved to the area hoping for a fresh start. Third, the Nebraska volunteer militia was sluggish. Having a lack of money did not help.

In 1881, the Nebraska Militia Act required mandatory drills. Successive days were required during the last month of summer. This every-other-year event was to help with field maneuvers and drills. Fifteen years later, new guidelines were passed for uniforms and expected behavior. All Nebraska troops had the same rules. Funding cuts did halt some plans. Lack of standards during the early guard years toughened them up and made them strive for improvement.

What really amped up training was the 1898 Spanish-American War. Nebraska was ready to go to war—at least they thought so, but orders from Washington had not arrived. Delays were beneficial, as this wait allowed troops to train longer.

The Nebraska/Lancaster County fairgrounds provided the perfect place to train, until Lincoln citizens decided to watch. Vendors even sold souvenirs. The streetcars arrived every fifteen minutes, and bicycles blocked roads. Finally, Lieutenant Stotsenburg declared, "no settlers, peddlers or hawkers" were allowed on grounds.

Other issues came to light. Officers were not fit enough to pass Lindell Hotel physicals. But the Third Nebraska Volunteer Infantry's involvement was affected the most. Someone famous affected their deployment.

William Jennings Bryan enlisted as a private. Governor Holcomb decided that was not fitting, so Colonel Bryan became unit commander. At least his assistant had a military background.

Nebraska units were sent to Cuba and to the Philippines. The third unit was sent to Florida. President McKinley did not want his former political opponent to become a war hero. When the Treaty of Paris was signed, Bryan resigned from the military. His campaign platform for the 1900 election was to fight against McKinley imperialism.

EARLY AVIATION

Captain Schaffer was chief of aviation and attempted to raise funds by flying at exhibitions. Too many accidents made him quit. Captain Ralph McMillen's barnstorming helped fund guard aviation. McMillen also experimented with weak bombs that exploded in midair. Since his targets were the capitol and penitentiary, the high detonations were recommended. Nebraska's early air guard ended when McMillen died in a 1916 exhibition.

STATE ARSENAL

17th and Court Streets

In 1912, Nebraska legislators determined that they should no longer store state explosives in the capitol. The original arsenal went up in 1913, and storage options greatly improved. Around this time, the guard was changing from the Nebraska Volunteer Militia to the present Nebraska National Guard. From 1963 to 1980, the Nebraska State Fair Board used the building for storage and security purposes.

The former state arsenal was near the railroad tracks where troops deployed. To name the activity center after Bob Devaney, the legislature had to overrule the law that stated buildings could not be named after living people. *Photo by the author.*

MUNICIPAL AIRPORT BEFORE WORLD WAR II

2400 West Adams Street

For the 1930 grand opening of the Municipal Airport, there were numerous "on to Lincoln" races. A year later, the airport was renamed Lindbergh Field. Around this time, five-and-a-half-hour flights were available to Chicago. For this $51.95 round-trip service, planes with heated cabins were available.

Twelve years later, the Lincoln Army Airfield took over the location. Aircraft mechanics and army aviation cadets needed a training location. This area helped troops get organized before heading overseas to fight. Flights brought troops back after the war. The city had its airport back at the end of 1945.

LINCOLN ARMY AIR FIELD REGIMENTAL CHAPEL
4601 Northwest 48th Street

At the beginning of World War II, the United States was keeping an eye on Europe. Although not a part of the war yet, President Roosevelt declared a "limited national emergency." Construction of military posts began. With universal designs and prefabricated materials, crews were able to travel the country to ready locations.

Mrs. Roosevelt insisted that churches be part of the plans. To improve morale, she felt military gathering places were needed. Soon, New England–style churches were being built on bases. From start to finish, Lincoln's chapel took three weeks to build. It held 362 seats. Beyond the sanctuary, additional spaces included the balcony, nursery and cloakroom. Offices, including one for the chaplain, were near the sanctuary. North of the building was Huskerville, and this section contained a fire station and hospital. This was one of the rare buildings not torn down after the war. During the time of the air force base, the chapel still served.

Across Nebraska, eleven army airfields were built according to plan once the United States entered the war. Less than four months after construction started, the base was open. The three-thousand-acre site was operational 150 days later at a cost of $15 million. In this time, more than one thousand buildings went up. During the three years of operation, twenty-five thousand aircraft mechanics and forty thousand aviators were trained in Lincoln.

AIR FORCE BASE
Lincoln's Air Park Area

Lincoln was not ready to be done with the military. The city convinced a naval reserve air station to become a part of Lincoln. Lincoln appealed to the Strategic Air Command (SAC) in Omaha to use Lincoln as a secondary location. The presentation was persuasive. Yet many steps needed to happen first.

Tenants had moved into facilities on the former base. Warehouse storage and manufacturing plants were busy. Guard units and aviation associations were still flying on location. The Naval Reserve Project, once celebrated, was now a complication. Due to budget cuts, the navy left town.

The air reserve moved over. Nearby Union Airport was expanded for commercial flight. Funds were raised to help private planes operate. In 1952, the Strategic Air Command activated the airfield as Lincoln Air Force Base

Not only is this the only army airfield regimental chapel left in Nebraska, but it is also one of few still standing across the United States. *Photo by the author.*

under a joint-use lease agreement between the U.S. Air Force and the City of Lincoln. Bomber wings, air refueling squadrons and an Atlas ICBM squadron were assigned to the base.

Although many of the army airfield buildings were less than a decade old, the air force base started over. To solve the housing crisis, comfortable dormitories were built instead of barracks. Officers had private baths. Recreation areas were supported by soldiers.

Families also needed places to stay. Local real estate did not like the lower-priced homes the base intended to build. The base overrode concerns, stating that security was at stake. In a crisis, personnel needed to be nearby.

Arnold Heights neighborhood began. A Nebraska senator impacted the base by funding housing. The Wherry Military Act allowed for the first four hundred ranch homes. The next addition was named after Indiana senator Capehart.

Beyond housing, the base needed headquarters, repair and firefighting facilities, along with buildings to store fuel and ammunition. Concrete paved the way for runways and apron parking. The Lincoln location became an important part of the Cold War defense system.

Troops had to be ready to perform a nuclear attack against the Soviet Union and other Communist countries. Numerous hours were spent learning how to aim bombs. To break up the boredom, the SAC had competitions. To get the best score, squads competed against one another. Not only did these events improve morale, they also kept troops motivated to continue training. Certain bomber crews had to be ready to fly right away. Atlas and Nike satellite installations were part of the landscape.

Having the base in town impacted Lincoln. At the Aqua-Air Show, airmen demonstrated their skills. Television star Andy Devine came to host. On the manmade Bowling Lake, a water show was impressive. The air force Thunderbirds performance squad also came to town.

For Lincoln's centennial a year later, the base held an open house. Tankers and bombers planned flyovers. This event connected local residents to the military community. The local United Service Organizations provided troops with a place to go. Some families "adopted" soldiers by asking them over for a meal or to attend church.

The base's arrival may have decreased Lincoln segregation. The military did not allow separation, and to help the base crowd feel comfortable, the community was encouraged to welcome everyone everywhere.

As Cold War threats diminished, the military was backing off. Across Lincoln, many were concerned about the air force base closing. Scores of articles were written about all of the possible economic pitfalls. Despite not receiving tax funding, Air Park is one of the largest industrial parks in the United States.

One particular twelve-year-old, Mike, could see a potential benefit. He wrote a letter to commander base colonel Joseph J. McLachlan. He inquired about buying and moving the little jet (by the wrecked B47) to his house.

Since the plane was grounded anyway, he did not think it would cause any trouble. Having an air force jet in his backyard would have been a hit with his friends. Sadly, Mike's dream did not come true. The fire department may have purchased the plane for crash and rescue practice.

Lincoln Air Force Base closed in 1966. Determining what the city would do with the all of the buildings and houses was one worry. Ultimately, Lincoln determined that public housing and larger commercial businesses were a good fit.

LINCOLN MUNICIPAL AIRPORT (FORMERLY THE AIR FORCE BASE)

2400 West Adams Street

When the Air Force left, Lincoln regained its airspace. The Lincoln Airport Authority took over operations of both the runaways and the former base. At one time, there was talk of building a large airport in between Lincoln and Omaha. Instead, a new terminal was built in 1976. Corten steel, which weathers naturally, was used as the core building material. If the airport ever wanted to expand, there is space for a second terminal.

In 1986, a Lincoln salesman's briefcase did not arrive on the plane. He filed a claim. When the case arrived, someone was overly vigilant and

Suspended from the Lincoln Municipal Airport ceiling is an Arrow Sport plane manufactured in Havelock in August 1929. *Photo by the author.*

113

blew it up without checking for claims. While there have been other issues through the years, Lincoln is thankful to not have any major incidents or crashes in its history.

The smaller Lincoln airport is known for extending hospitality. Many Husker team welcome-back parties have happened through the years. Some even show up for the opposing team arrivals. Since 2002, the Red Coats offer reassurance to travelers by listening and directing them where they need to go.

OAK CREEK PARK

1459 Sun Valley Boulevard

Oak Creek Park had become a rubbish dump. To clean up the land, every year, ten to fifteen acres were filled with waste and then sodded over. Soon, the former Salt Creek dump became Oak Creek Park.

By 1927, numerous trees and shrubs were being planted. This Stewart Tract was supposed to be the new baseball park, but the four planned baseball diamonds were never built. Today, many continue to enjoy boating on the lake. On July 3, this park now hosts Uncle Sam Jam, including fireworks.

SPEEDWAY MOTORS

340 Victory Lane

"Speedy" Bill Smith opened Speedway Motors, one of the Midwest's first speed shops, in 1952. Within a decade, his company was manufacturing fiberglass hot rod bodies and speed parts for both hot rodders and racers. Speedway became quickly involved in many forms of racing throughout the United States and was very successful. In 1992, the Museum of American Speed, a 501 c-3 nonprofit museum, opened to showcase Bill's world-class collections.

CAPITOL BEACH

The finest amusement park in the Western country, band concerts and other excellent attractions are provided afternoons and evenings throughout the summer months.

—*Capitol Beach 1913 brochure*

When Lancaster was not yet Lincoln, the Gregory Basin salt flats were sprawling. Investors developed Burlington Beach at this site. Near the manmade lake, a pavilion allowed for dancing and meetings. The *Belle of the Blue* steamboat provided rides for fifty people. In 1892, the crowd was noted to be around fifty thousand.

This area was renamed Capitol Beach in 1906. Hundreds of trees were planted. Several crowd pleasers were added to the property, including Casino Moving Pictures Theater (1913), a midsized Midway (1920), a saltwater swimming pool (1926) and the King's Ballroom (1937).

One of the investors was William Ferguson. At one time, in 1915, the city almost bought the property for recreational purposes. The lake was drained and refilled several times. Today, private homes are built around the lake.

For several decades, Capitol Beach was the place where Lincoln went for entertainment. The amusement park, which operated for over fifty years, was a big draw. *Author Stephanie Grace Whitson's collection.*

6

FAIRVIEW, NORMAL AND COLLEGE VIEW

This area was once farmland. Outside the city limits, views presented wide-open possibilities. Like its locations, their history would be absorbed into Lincoln.

FAIRVIEW

4900 Sumner Street

Here at Fairview we expect to spend the remainder of our days except such time as may be devoted to travel. Here the children can find fresh air and healthy exercise; here I can indulge my taste for farming; here, too, the friends who are passing this midway point between the oceans can find a welcome and a word of cheer.

—*William Jennings Bryan*

A side trip to see an old college friend changed the course of William Jennings Bryan's life. Adolphus Talbot practiced law in Lincoln, and Bryan liked the feel of the town. With his family, he decided to relocate. In 1877, Bryan arrived in Lincoln first. His family followed several months later. Mary Bryan's parents helped them purchase their first Lincoln home at 1625 D Street. Its multiple porches and balconies provided perfect platforms for Bryan to speak.

Bryan soon took on a public role. Twenty thousand populists attended a Cushman Park rally. Soon after, he was elected to Congress. As the *Omaha*

World-Herald editor, he practiced refining his policies. In his own paper, the *Commoner*, he wrote for the American laborer and farmer.

At thirty-six, he became the youngest presidential candidate. He was also one of the first to run from west of the Mississippi. He ran unsuccessfully for president three times. He also ran unsuccessfully for Presbyterian General Assembly monitor three times. Despite not being elected, he was well liked and popular. During his campaigns, he talked to a staggering number of people on America's first whistle-stop tour. For the Methodist Chautauqua assemblies, he was a popular, frequent speaker.

In 1901, the Bryans built a country home east of Lincoln. Profits from his books paid for the property. Over time, the Bryans had purchased a few hundred acres along Antelope Creek. Designed by Artemus Roberts, Fairview was named for the panorama provided from the top of the hill. Bryan's goal was for his home to be the Monticello of the West—a gathering place for democracy. Frequently, the community was invited for both political assemblies and outdoor get-togethers. When the days of presidential speeches were over in 1908, the chilly front porch was enclosed.

Rudolph Evans's first sculpture of William Jennings Bryan became part of Stautory Hall in 1937. Evans created another sculpture of Bryan that was temporarily placed in cement at the Nebraska capitol. Today, Bryan's likeness is back in front of his former home, Fairview. *Photo by the author.*

Due to Mary's poor health, the Bryans relocated to Florida. He offered ten acres and Fairview to his Presbyterian church for a hospital. It declined. Since his mother had been a Methodist, he tried that denomination next. Lincoln Methodist Hospital soon opened. When he died in 1925, the name was changed to Bryan Memorial Hospital. Fairview sat directly east of the new building and became a home for student nurses for several years.

The Junior League and Nebraska State Historical Society worked together to restore Fairview to its original condition in 1961. Since little remained of the Bryans' personal belongings, the house is considered a period restoration. Photographs were consulted, so the house reflects the original feel. Three years later, the house became a national historic landmark. Surrounded by Bryan Hospital and the city of Lincoln, the views are no longer quite as stunning.

NORMAL HEIGHTS

In 1892, Normal Heights started a post office that would outlast the village. Located three miles southeast of Lincoln, the location was perfect for a new type of training college. Although the town never incorporated, this part of town is still considered Normal.

Normal University
Near 56th and South Streets
Teacher training schools were once called "normal schools." Artemus Roberts designed this sturdy structure to "stand the wear and tear of centuries." By year two, almost six hundred students attended. Students could start school at any point. Only eighteen weeks and twenty-four dollars were required for certification.

The university may have lasted for years. But when flames destroyed the fireproof main building, it closed. To build South Ward High School, the city purchased part of the property. That school was open less than thirty years. Dr. Benjamin Bailey bought the rest of the former university property.

Roberts Park
1822 South 56th Street
Artemus Roberts lived with his family near Normal. His son began making home deliveries of milk produced by his herd of sixty cows, which led to the

All that is left of the former Normal College are the capstones that are now displayed (and climbed on) at Roberts Park. *Photo by the author.*

start of Roberts Dairy. In 1933, J.R. and his wife gave the city the former family apple orchard. Within a year, trees were cleaned up and planted. At one time, a rock pool was a part of the landscape.

Green Gables Sanatorium/Madonna Rehabilitation Hospital
52nd and South Streets

Dr. Bailey thought people lived longer in Lincoln. He decided to capitalize on youthfulness by starting a sanatorium southeast of Lincoln. According to Dr. Bailey, Lincoln was the perfect size and location at the ideal altitude of 1,200 feet. Lincoln enjoyed "freedom from fogs, perpetual sunshine and a country that is one of the garden spots of the earth."

While Bailey sounded like a salesman, he was qualified to help. He practiced medicine for several years. He also presided over the state board of health and worked with homeopathic societies. He wanted to ease the pain of those suffering from chronic noncontagious sicknesses.

The former Normal University female dorm became the Saint James building. At the sanatorium, options included elaborate baths, masseurs, physical instructors, a fine gymnasium and a billiard room. Both cereal products and trendy hygienic foods were served. Turkish rooms and guest lodging added to the appeal.

In 1958, the Benedictine Sisters of Yankton bought the sanatorium grounds. They wanted to care for the elderly at their Madonna facility. Within a decade, they added rehabilitation services. In 1971, a new short-term residence was constructed. Five years later, the last of the Normal University buildings was torn down. For more than sixty years, Madonna Rehabilitation Hospital has been helping patients recover from injuries.

UNION COLLEGE AND COLLEGE VIEW
48th–52nd Streets between Calvert and Prescott Streets

The Seventh-day Adventist Battle Creek Michigan College was overcrowded. Seven midwestern towns were trying to host the next school. Despite the bitterly cold weather during its visit, the committee liked Lincoln. Land was offered to the group to build businesses and the school. As the property was outside of the city, noise and smoke would be limited—so would the evils of society. Union College was coming to Nebraska.

To start the process, Enoch Jenkins hiked through five miles of snow to construct the tool house. The Sisley Barn, which became the first office, hotel and meetinghouse, was built next. While that barn is gone, the 1890 Eno house is still standing at the same 3919 South Forty-Eighth Street property. Mrs. Sisley may have been the busiest of all, as she took care of everything from payroll to nursing to entertaining. Professor Prescott wanted to do something to say thank you, and Mr. Sisley suggested a subscription to *Ladies Home Journal*.

Two thousand dollars was given by the City of Lincoln for an electric street line to the college. Before, horse-drawn carts had only traveled to Twenty-Seventh, and a three-mile hike was necessary to get to campus. Early riders remember that when crossing the Thirty-Second and Sheridan tracks "penny bridge," one cent was required to continue to either Lincoln or College View.

In August 1891, visitors were excited to see the new campus. Electric trains were attached to transport visitors. But on the hill heading toward campus, the cars got stuck when there was not enough electricity in the line to continue. Each car had to be disconnected and then driven separately.

The Lincoln mayor welcomed the college. People picnicked while a band played. Guests were taken to the top of the buildings to see the breathtaking views. For the September 1891 dedication day, there was a similar welcome. When the opera chairs had not arrived, the crowd sat on planks. A quartet from the Lincoln Music Conservatory played the strings.

Opening day of the college turned rainy and sad. After a young teacher died unexpectedly one week after his wedding, the funeral happened that first night. Students were homesick already. "Home Sweet Home" at the impromptu program was depressing. Popcorn and "Pop Goes the Weasel" might have saved the school that night.

After classes, students marched in unison to chapel or to their next classes. A music student played the piano, which caused the whole building to shake. Silence was enforced. Later, a bell was used to change classes.

At the start, students could learn in Scandinavian languages. At first, dorms, Sabbath schools and churches were all segregated based on nation of origin, as national culture was important during the early years. A bigger concern, though, was separating the boys and girls. Although both were housed in the same dorm, a double staircase kept the groups apart. Talking to one another was limited to calling hours. When the staff realized that the post office was a meeting place, mail was delivered on campus. Policies did not change for a long time.

Torn down decades ago, these original Union College buildings were used for administration, classrooms and residences. This circa 1900 picture was purchased from Union College. *Author's collection.*

Each student had one chair. To sit for dining or in the prayer room, students carried that chair with them. Commodes, slop jars and kerosene were part of the early days. Around the campus, students wore galoshes to combat an abundance of mud. Students did not complain. They considered themselves to be pioneers.

Tuition was only fifteen dollars per month. Light, heat, simple laundry and two meals were covered. Dining ended at 1:30 p.m. At first, only fruit was allowed for snacks. Graham crackers made in the bakery became another exception. Farm kids struggled to adjust to limited meals and city life. Parents shipped broncos to their homesick kids. Soon there was an ordinance against horse riding in town.

Part of Union College's emphasis was teaching children how to work. Six hours of weekly domestic work were required. The broom shop, print shop, tailoring, pecanery and bookbindery were also potential jobs. Lack of student motivation ended the work policy in the 1930s.

J.H. Kellogg of Battle Creek, Michigan, started the Nebraska Sanitarium in 1895. Achieving overall health was his goal. One contest he set up allowed the best morally and physically fit students to get a free year of tuition. At the clinic students could steam or boil away illnesses.

In the early days, College View did not have a bank, and taking the funds to Lincoln every day was challenging. Since the school and village transactions happened at the college, thousands of dollars were often on hand. "Uncle Joe" Sutherland, the business manager, and M.W. Newton, the accountant, divided the money and took it home to their connecting row houses. To keep the money safe, they rigged switches and alarms between the houses. One night, Mrs. Sutherland set off the alarm. Thankfully, that was the only time the alarm was ever triggered.

Candy to eat
Gum to chew
And roasted peanuts
From College View

Around the turn of the twentieth century, more Seventh-day Adventists were becoming vegetarian. To support their diets, alternative proteins like peanuts became important. As Dave Weiss imported southern goobers to sell, he became known as the peanut man. At Sunday baseball games, boys acted as his vendors. Trolleys filled with riders came to town to buy the nuts. This is how Union College became known as peanut hill. A later grocery store was named for the tradition.

To save money and teach industry, the school operated a farm. Crops were pickled, sugar beets were served and corn became fuel. Poultry mattered. For misbehaving students, nighttime watermelon harvesting was discipline.

The "Golden Cord" tradition honors the Adventist missionaries around the globe. On a large map, a ribbon connected Lincoln and the mission field locations. Today, a map visualizes the places where students are changing the world. As the school says, "Union never forgets her own."

Union College Schools
5240/5140 Calvert Street

For students who were not ready for college level classes, prep classes were initially offered. In 1924, Union College Academy started to become independent but met on campus until 1963. At today's College View Academy, the mission to "nurture Christ and serve humanity" has continued. Next door is the Helen Hyatt Elementary School. For years, the younger children met in Old East Hall. Hyatt, a former African missionary, was principal of the training school. This location is the site of the former dairy.

Christian Record Company
3705 South 48ᵗʰ Street (Now 5900 South 58ᵗʰ Street)

One of the Seventh-day Adventist ministries is a braille publishing house. In 1904, the business moved to Lincoln. A 1930s Art Deco building was constructed to house more equipment. Spaces included a library, stereotype room for braille printing plates and a press room. On the top floor were offices and a large, two-bedroom apartment.

Although now it is at a new location, Christian Record has been producing books and magazines for the blind for over 120 years.
Photo by the author.

In 1965, the company moved out, and Capital City Bookbindery moved in. Today, Christian Record operates in southeast Lincoln and is considered the largest braille religious publisher in the world. From books to talking magazines, every publication is complimentary for the blind. Today, inside this historic building is Union Bank offices.

College View

At first, College View consisted of covered wagons and tents. Starting a village meant organizing everything from government to sidewalks. For fire protection, citizens used pails and ladders. A locked fire house did not stop people from borrowing equipment and forgetting to return it. Wandering or even improperly tethered animals were impounded. Farmers were not fans of that policy.

Town rules reflected the conservative college. All those under the age of twenty-one had a 9:00 p.m. curfew. Bikes were not allowed on streets. Even the streetcars could not travel faster than ten miles per hour at first. A 1916 law stated, "It shall be unlawful for any person to maintain or operate any public pool hall, billiard hall, bowling alley, picture show, theatrical or vaudeville entertainment, roller skating rink, swimming pool, merry-go-round, circus, dancing pavilion or other place of public amusement for pay in the village of College View, Nebraska." Over time, the laws lessened.

The community lumberyard had the town phone. Six lines were connected. To further communicate with the outside world, teachers added two hundred drops for additional phone lines.

From the beginning, Lincoln wanted College View to become part of the town. By 1912, College View had its own waterworks. Four years later, it added the library and city hall. During the 1920s, the community voted three times before deciding on annexation in 1929, at which point 2,500 people became part of Lincoln. Certain citizens were still skeptical, but police and fire protection improved—so did the streets, sidewalks and the water supply.

Adventist Book Store Today
4745 Prescott Avenue

Zalmon Nicola's general store was a lifeline for the early town. It was a store and a location to pick up mail, and upstairs was even the first location of the Sabbath school.

Later, a dentist office was at this location, and books were stacked in the corner for the first town library—for a day anyway, as the building burned that night. A professor donated books again. But in 1903, the building burned again. At this point, the town worked on organizing a different library.

Other buildings occupied the land. Then the college was thrilled to be able to buy such a significant property. Today, the Adventist Book Center is housed here.

Bank of College View
Formerly 4728 Prescott Avenue

At first, the school controlled the money for the town. The Bank of College View served the town for several years before Farmer's State Bank took over. The Great Depression caused the downfall of that bank too.

Although times were tough, W.E. Barkley, president of the Union Life Insurance Company, reorganized the bank. He even gave back a percentage to those who lost money in the previous failed bank. In June 1930, the name was changed to Union Bank. While many branches have opened, the main headquarters is still near Forty-Eighth and Bancroft.

College View Public Library
3800 South 48th Street

Since previous attempts at a library had burned, rented rooms were the town's best option. After collecting more than 1,500 volumes, the time had come for a building. College View asked Andrew Carnegie for $7,500. The beautiful buff brick building that was constructed added class to the corner.

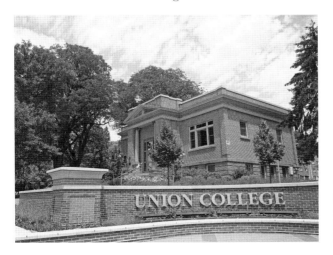

This former College View Carnegie library is now used for Union College Communications and Publicity. *Photo by the author.*

During its fifty-six years of operation, it had only three librarians. Gere Library replaced this city branch in 1971. This historic building is part of Union College today.

College View Seventh-day Adventist Church
4801 Prescott Avenue
In 1894, College View was ready for a Seventh-day Adventist Church. A 2,000-seat auditorium was requested. Using the college chapel or gymnasium no longer worked well. Although money was tight in 1894, the church opened almost debt free. Both locals and the conference funded the building.

Ninety years later, the church needed a new building. The sanctuary design was fan-shaped for better acoustics. Some of the former stained-glass windows hang in the lobby area. Two new upper windows in the sanctuary tell the Adventist story. But the most magnificent stained-glass windows are the ones that stretch across the hallway. From Eden to the second coming, the Bible story is presented in images.

Alice's Restaurant
4013 South 48th Street
First called a café, this restaurant once had three locations. As the oldest of six kids, Alice cooked meals and during harvest. After moving to Lincoln, she started her first restaurant in 1958. Lines were often out the door. Favorites were apple fritters and the complimentary cinnamon raisin bread.

Cedar Lawn Memorial Park
Seventieth Street and Pioneers Boulevard
East of town, the college owned ten acres. This became the community cemetery in 1903. Today, the Nebraska Conference owns the location. Several prominent town members are buried here.

Holmes Park
Seventieth Street and Normal Boulevard
From early Lincoln days, Salt Creek and its tributaries caused havoc in Lincoln. From 1881 to 1885, there were seventeen major floods. Countless homes and businesses were damaged in the area. Some lives were even lost.

University graduate Otto Liebers called his neighbors together. To stop the flooding, the Upper Salt Creek farmers needed to work together. This group changed Lincoln. Channels were redirected, and the flooding was minimized. Lieber's life was changed as he became president of Salt Valley Watershed and later became a representative for state legislature district 18 to pass laws regarding watersheds. Holmes Lake was part of the solution and has saved Lincoln from many floods since 1963.

House of Flowers
6940 Van Dorn Street
Lincoln's oldest flower shop started downtown in 1903 and was known as Hiltner Brothers Florists. The "Florists" portion was changed to "House of Flowers" in 1970. For many years, the florist operated out of the former Townshend Studio near Eleventh and M. While owners have changed through the years, its flowers still brighten Lincoln faces.

7

SOUTH LINCOLN

GERMANS FROM RUSSIA

For only eight dollars, Volga Germans arrived in Lincoln by train. Due to hardships, these Germans had moved to Russia only to be forced to relocate again later. Sociologist Hattie Plum Williams noted, "The Russian Germans in Lincoln are settled chiefly along the west edge of the city, in two compact groups, separated from each other and from the rest of the city by the railroad yards and wholesale district." Since communities often immigrated together, the *Ivergasse* ("uptown") and *Unnergass* ("downtown") reflected previous Russian settlements and upbringings.

Early summers were spent in Nebraska beet fields. In the winter, they lived in the "Rooshen" creek bottoms. Railroad land was accessible and inexpensive. Frequent floods did not deter them.

By 1914, these citizens formed one-third of Lincoln's population. *Die Welt Post* printed news from the homeland. Churches, a school and even a bank operated in German. But World War I changed the climate. Speaking German in schools was forbidden, and strong Germans were investigated. Eight university professors were examined for treason, and three were forced to resign.

But these communities continued on and contributed to Lincoln's heritage. Sam Schwartzkopf became mayor of Lincoln, and his brother Ed was UNL regent. After his Husker career, George Sauer played for the Green Bay Packers. He coached several university teams.

NORTH BOTTOMS

Both Salt Creek and the university kept this settlement smaller. Students attended Z Street School. Z Street became Charleston Street. The school was renamed Hayward in honor of a Nebraska City lawyer/farmer/stock breeder who died while serving in the Senate. Since 1981, condos have occupied the former school.

German Evangelical Congregational Salem Church formed in 1901 at 915 Charleston Street. Due to lower neighborhood numbers, it merged with nearby Evangelical Saint John's in 1966. They became Faith United Church of Christ. Numbers continued to decline. The last service in 2009 included a symbolic ringing of the bells. Now the historic building is home to Redeemer Presbyterian. The former Saint John's Church (1324 New Hampshire) has been home to many other congregations.

Immanuel Church is still connected to these early settlers. In 1891, thirteen people started Immanuel German Reformed Church. In 1916, it built at Tenth and Charleston. This is the "church with the lighted cross."

SOUTH BOTTOMS

FIRST GERMAN CONGREGATIONAL CHURCH/FIRST BIBLE

100 West F Street

After meeting at Park School in 1888, Germans formed a church. Because the first building was too close to the railroad, it relocated after World War I. With shovels in hand, the congregation dug out the next building and helped with construction. Until 1975, part of the service was done in German.

In 2009, this congregation asked Faith Bible Church for help with revitalization. Faith's proposal involved sending a pastor, leadership team and members. First German accepted. The name was changed to First Bible to reflect the new movement.

FRIEDEN'S LUTHERAN CHURCH

540 D Street

Aside from holding church services since 1907, *Frieden*, which means "peace" in German, offered citizenship classes and community events. Certain services were conducted in German into the 1960s. One tradition continues: before a funeral, the bells ring once for every year that the person lived.

Built in the style of a Volga Russian church, Frieden's Lutheran had two domes until a 1925 fire altered the building. *Photo by the author.*

GERMAN EVANGELICAL CONGREGATIONAL ZION CHURCH, ZION PCA

1035 South 9th Street

Around 1900, this German church met at 425 F Street. Wanting more room, the church relocated to Ninth and D Streets in 1927. Fifty years later, Covenant Presbyterian merged with that dwindling congregation to form Zion PCA.

Two days before the church was to break ground on an educational wing, Zion burned to the ground. The eighty-year-old church was gone. Much was lost, including the David Monrose mural of heavenly new Jerusalem. A bell, a few pews, many stained-glass windows and the cornerstone, which included a German letter from the original building committee, were saved. Today, Zion PCA is at the former Southwood Lutheran location at 5511 South Twenty-Seventh Street.

EBENEZER CONGREGATIONAL

801 B Street

In 1915, the Zion pastor left to start a new Volga Church farther south. During the early years, the building was small enough that fruit trees also covered the property. Its 1927 building features arts-and-craft-style stained-glass windows created by Lincoln Art Glass Works.

AMERICAN HISTORICAL SOCIETY OF GERMANS FROM RUSSIA

631 D Street

This former home is the national headquarters for this displaced group of people. Not only is the Lincoln Russian Bottoms history preserved, but this national organization also celebrates the nationwide contributions of Germans from Russia. Research rooms are available, and artifacts displayed in the museum illustrate history. During warmer months, the historic outbuildings tell even more of the story.

During the summer of 2019, Serving Hands celebrated fifty years of campus life in Lincoln. This sculpture, *Mark of a Great Nation*, by artist Jill Mulligan was in front of the American Historical Society of Germans from Russia. *Photo by the author.*

COOPER PARK

6th and D Streets

At first, city officials did not have time to develop the eleven acres set aside for recreation. Until 1889, this location supplied millions of gallons of city water. Eventually, trees established this park. Through the years, this spot has been known as Lincoln, Capitol, F Street and First City Park.

The brick picnic shelter plaque, "Joseph Cooper, He Loved Children," is in honor of the 1951 Cooper Foundation gift. Nearby, Nebraskan Sondra Johnson's statue *Daydreams* is reminiscent of Dorothy and her dog, Toto. This *Wonderful Wizard of Oz* reference is purposeful. William Jennings Bryan, author Frank Baum's friend, held many political rallies in the park. Some think the book is a political parody starring Bryan as the Tin Man.

Still standing next to its replacement, this 1873 small white building near Thirteenth and F is Lincoln's oldest standing church. *Photo by the author.*

LINCOLN'S LONGEST STANDING CHURCH
1302 F Street

With denomination mergers and reorganizing, Saint Paul's was Evangelical, Lutheran, Reformed, Congregational and Christian. The church began in February 1873 and came to its end on Easter 2014. Numbers had dwindled through the years. Today, F Street Community Church meets in the building and continues the mission of changing this neighborhood.

MT. ZION BAPTIST CHURCH
1205 F Street/3301 North 56th Street

At least four early founders of this 1879 church were from Louisiana. Growth happened when workers came to Lincoln for construction and railroad jobs. Some were educated in other fields but struggled to find certain jobs in

Lincoln. One Missouri teacher became a barber when African American teachers were not allowed.

An 1892 merger with Second Baptist allowed a larger church to be constructed at Twelfth and F Streets. It stayed for over a century. When the congregation moved out, Lincoln Baptist Church moved in. Mt. Zion personalized its new northeast location. Rodney Scott of Architectural Glassarts created stained-glass windows to reflect African American heritage.

QUINN CHAPEL AFRICAN METHODIST EPISCOPAL CHURCH
1225 South 9th Street

Lincoln's first African American congregation started in 1871. African Americans lived in this neighborhood until some groups moved to Twentieth and T Streets near campus. This building was moved from another location and then expanded.

The Last Supper was once in the sanctuary front but did not connect with the congregation. Longtime member and Doane University professor Marilyn Johnson-Farr commissioned her artist friend to create a mural to reflect the community's heritage. Jesus is shown with outstretched arms to welcome African Americans.

SAINT FRANCIS OF ASSISI
1145 South Street

This church was once considered a part of Saint Elizabeth Hospital before it relocated. The stained-glass windows are notable. Catholics still gather in this chapel.

MOORE HOUSE/HAZEL ABEL PARK
1840 East Street

The Moore brothers made money in loans and real estate. Robert was once mayor, legislator and lieutenant governor. The Moores deeded their house to Lincoln General Hospital, which sold it to fund other projects. The house became a nursery school and then a Girls Scouts headquarters before being purchased by the Abel Foundation.

George Abel owned concrete companies. His wife, Hazel, was a teacher and later a temporary senator. Near the end of World War II, Hazel wanted to help military families. The House of Hospitality opened in the former Moore house for deployed soldiers' families.

In the 1960s, the house was torn down. The Abels gave the land to Lincoln. Alice wanted to honor her mother's memory with a park. Renaissance fences were added to the initial green space, and an English gazebo filled one corner. Mounted in the donated fountain is a two-hundred-year-old cherub centerpiece that Hazel purchased in Paris.

FIRST PRESBYTERIAN
840 South 17th Street

Intending to be a Montana missionary, Reverend Peck stayed in Lincoln to help start First Presbyterian. The Eleventh and J Street frame church had a square tower. Money was tight, so to raise funds, leadership tried a pew rental system and paid solicitors to raise subscriptions for donations.

With six hundred members, the congregation built at the southwest corner of Thirteenth and M. Both President Wilson and presidential candidate Calvin Coolidge visited the church. When the property was sold for the Cornhusker Hotel, the church needed to relocate.

Andrew and Winona Sawyer were early settlers. His Lincoln Floral Conservatory at Seventeenth and G was possibly the biggest greenhouse west of the Mississippi. By using a hot water heating system, their flowers survived Lincoln's climate. Notable in her own right, Winona was the third Nebraska woman to pass the bar exam.

The Sawyers hosted a citywide New Year's Eve celebration when Andrew was mayor in 1887 and 1888. As a circuit court chancery and state senator, he remained involved until his leg was amputated in 1916. That same year, Sawyer compiled Lincoln's history into a notable two-volume series. When he died in 1924, Winona sold their property to the church for $20,000.

Gothic expert Ralph Adams Cram, a former Goodhue associate, worked with local Davis Design on the church. One distinct feature is the twin bell towers. Keats Lorenz completed several original oak carvings.

FIRST-PLYMOUTH CONGREGATIONAL CHURCH
20ᵗʰ and D Streets

On lots given them by the state, First Congregational Church built one of Lincoln's first churches. A decade later, it built a larger church at Thirteenth and L. After the property sold for the Cornhusker Hotel, it combined with the church plant Plymouth Congregational. For five years, the congregation met at the Seventeenth and A Street church until it outgrew the building

To have enough land, the church purchased and tore down the Whitten-Carlise School. Three architects sent proposals. Harold Van Buren Magonigle lost the capitol competition, but this time, his design was chosen over Goodhue's plan. As an early U.S. architecture doctoral graduate, Magonigle's resume was impressive.

The design reflected Nebraska. For the six shades of bricks, rose and tawny gold symbolized the sunset sky and harvest fields. According to legend, the church represented a manor farm with the bell tower appearing like a silo, but no written proof has verified this.

As seen from the capitol, this is First-Plymouth Church. Both buildings are considered two of Nebraska's finest. *Photo by the author.*

Plymouth, England, sent a stone from a 1619 pilgrims' house before the Mayflower. Former president and Plymouth, Vermont native, Calvin Coolidge chose the inscription. Eisleben, Germany, also sent a stone from Martin Luther's birth home. Both are at the base of Nebraska's first carillon tower.

Carillons are a type of bell played by striking keys and pedals. Forty-eight bells were cast in England and sent to the church. One of the nation's finest carillon players debuted the bells at a May 30, 1931 concert. Nearby streets filled with around twenty-five thousand people. Sixty years later, more bells were added. Now, fifty-seven bells are played at the start of many services.

WESTMINSTER PRESBYTERIAN
2110 Sheridan Boulevard

In 1892, Second Presbyterian started a mission Sunday school. The church planting efforts resulted in Pleasant Hill Chapel, later renamed "Westminster." The church moved a few times. In 1922, it purchased land on the edge of Lincoln.

Westminster Presbyterian's west sanctuary window is a replica of a window from the Stratford-on-Avon Shakespeare Memorial Church. *Photo by the author.*

Westminster reached out to Lincoln's newer neighborhood. In February, Dorothy Frasier would host the Azalea Silver Tea. She filled her south Lincoln home with luxurious flowers and then offered tours to the formally dressed ladies. After the high tea, Frasier took a freewill silver offering to help the church.

One of the best purchases the church made was a fine Skinner organ. Choirs were formed for singers and boy bell ringers. When trolleys still operated from South Street to Sheridan, they stopped near the church on Christmas Eve. The girl choir sang from the balcony while the director played the portable organ. Trolley passes were given so patrons could stay and listen.

JEWISH CONGREGATIONS

The first Jewish settlers arrived in Lincoln around 1867. Although the Jews must have connected, no official congregations started until 1884. Both the early temple and synagogue are still around today. While some of their Lincoln history overlaps, there are distinctions in beliefs.

Temple of Congregation B'Nai Jeshuran
2061 South 20th Street

In October 1884, five Jewish men organized this Reformed Jewish synagogue. Although land was acquired at Twelfth and D in 1885, the church was incomplete for eight years. Membership was slow to grow. When the first temple caught fire in 1922, the group chose to relocate south rather than rebuild.

In the new temple, Byzantine elements included geometric shapes. Exterior details include the Star of David stained-glass window and the carved Ten Commandments. When the seats are filled, the octagonal dome roof design creates perfect sanctuary acoustics. Keats Lorenz carved the sanctuary's Ark of the Temple. This South Street Temple remains true to its roots.

Congregation Tifereth Israel
3219 Sheridan Boulevard

In 1910, the 1898 Congregation Talmud Torah (1898) merged with Congregation Tifereth Israel (1903). Until 1954, the synagogue was located in downtown Lincoln. *Tifereth* means "glory to." A synagogue is intended to be a house of study, prayer and worship.

This distinct Jewish synagogue is commonly called the South Street Temple. *Photo by the author.*

To picture Lincoln Jewish history, the stone scroll must be read from right to left. *Photo by the author.*

At the new location, Albert Woods and his five sons took six months to carve "The Doors to the Ark of the Covenant." The eight most important Jewish holidays are explained in the woodwork. To point Jews toward Jerusalem, these artistic doors are on the eastern wall.

Congregation member Max Neiden wanted a visual picture of Lincoln Jewish history. Jay Tschetter of Brickstone researched the mural, and then his brother, Dean, took the design lead. Dean had worked as a Walt Disney Imagineering consultant and won an Emmy Award for his art direction.

CATHEDRAL OF THE RISEN CHRIST
3500 Sheridan Boulevard

This parish started slowly in 1932 by renting a house for meetings. Twenty years later, there was a need for a school, but another decade passed before a church was built. By 1963, the diocese wanted the cathedral to be part of

Hungarian artist Giovanni Hajnal created this stone distic mosaic for the Holy Family Chapel in the Cathedral of the Risen Christ. Connections are made between the tree-planting Nebraska pioneers and Jesus, the carpenter's son. *Photo by the author.*

this parish. At the modern Cathedral of the Risen Christ, the resurrection is a predominant stained-glass theme. Possibly the only window with this theme worldwide, one distinct window features Jesus as a gardener near the empty tomb.

MEMORIAL PARK

33rd between South and Sheridan Streets

This section of Antelope Park was given to Lincoln by J.C. Seacrest. On either side of the drive, a tree was planted for every man killed in World War I. Markers placed by the Lincoln Woman's Club honored each life. This group also donated the *Pioneer Woman* cast concrete statue to Lincoln. Bess Streeter Aldrich's character from *A Lantern in her Hand* inspired sculptor Ellis Louis Burman.

COUNTRY CLUB OF LINCOLN

3200 South 24th Street

Lincoln's first golf course opened in 1900. A nearby house turned into a clubhouse, but then development came to Twenty-Seventh and A. The Lincoln Country Club moved and officially reorganized itself in 1903. Governor Butler's former mansion at Seventh and Washington made the perfect location. Forty acres allowed for a compact course. With the basement decorated like a dungeon, this was an intriguing place to visit.

In 1922, the Country Club of Lincoln, as it had been called for seventeen years, opened its new location. This space provided room to grow, and many members began building homes nearby. A community of connection has been created among the members, and it continues to last into the next century.

SEVENTEENTH STREET SHOPS

Near 17th and Sumner Streets

Wendelin's Bakery, located on nearby South Street, stored its delivery trucks here. Later, the garage was subdivided to become a costume shop and the Violin Shop. While the Grateful Bread has been serving up dough since 1998, this vegetarian spot took over a plumbing shop.

Several other commercial buildings have substantiated the neighborhood. Before Augustums Printing opened in 1965, it was the post office. Antique shops have been open for many years. On the corner was a five and dime known for sandwiches.

O-CONNELL-GALBRAITH HOUSE
727 South 9th Street

A variety of immigrants lived at one of Lincoln's oldest surviving brick houses. John Johnson, a prominent photographer in the local African American community, used this house as a backdrop for several of his pictures of community members. Currently, the building is home to a barbershop.

ROBBER'S CAVE
925 Robbers Cave Road

Two midwestern men hired Jacob Andra to work on their Lincoln brewery. To expand the cave to 5,600 feet of caverns took Andra about three years. Due to financial depression caused by drought and grasshoppers, the enterprise was short lived.

Rumors abound about the cave's use. Possibly that the Pawnee Council met here. Use as an Underground Railroad station is improbable since the cave is not near either a border or a river. While the cave was possibly named for Jesse James, proof that he hid inside has yet to be discovered. On its march to Washington, D.C., to protest soldier unemployment in 1884, Coxey's Army might have stopped here. As for ghost sightings, stories of viewers vary.

Confederate coins were found inside. The Scarboroughs, the longtime owners, kept coyotes on the property. Before opening picnic grounds, they started a mushroom garden. Whether the cave was officially open or not, young people found a way inside—so did secret societies, including the Ku Klux Klan. Through the years, this cave has connected the Lincoln community.

Starting in 1906, the curious paid money to explore. Today, visitors can reserve a guided tour led by local expert Joel Green. His book, *Robber's Cave: Truths, Legends, Recollections*, tells many more stories.

This original sandstone section of Robber's Cave was formed long before Lincoln. *Photo by the author.*

BEDIENT PIPE ORGAN

3300 South 6th Street

Gene Bedient started the Bedient Pipe Organ Company in 1969. First, he operated out of his garage before moving to the former Tiffereth Synagogue. For a time, organs were constructed in a former Air Park parachute factory.

The masterpiece Bedient organs are in many Lincoln churches. Two locations include Saint Paul United Methodist and First Christian Church. After Gene's retirement, the company continues to flourish with its tradition of integrity and high-quality work.

WILLARD COMMUNITY CENTER (FORMERLY WILLARD ELEMENTARY SCHOOL)

1245 South Folsom Street

In 1915, West A School was renamed to honor Frances Willard. Miss Willard was a Lincoln teacher who became Northwestern University dean of women in 1873. Through speeches, she supported temperance unions. Formerly used for education, the building is now used for connection. In particular, youth and the elderly can find a place to belong.

YANKEE HILL BRICK MANUFACTURING COMPANY

3705 South Coddington Avenue

Joseph Stockwell began making bricks in 1881. He discovered a stock of shale southwest of the city. Early beehive-style kilns are still on the property. Some older stacks are octagonal. In 1955, the tunnel kiln was introduced. One of Lincoln's first businesses became the city's biggest brick supplier.

RUNZA

Formerly near 1st and West Van Dorn Street

Two iconic restaurants started in this southwest area. Although the original 1949 Runza near First and Van Dorn is gone, this Lincoln original has several dozen fast food locations. Runza's foundation is known as *bierocks* in old German cookbooks. This distinct sandwich includes a spiced hamburger and cabbage mix baked inside dough.

LEE'S CHICKEN

1940 West Van Dorn Street

Lee's did not start as a chicken place. After taking over a small restaurant, Lee and Alice Frank needed more customers. Making French fries intrigued Alice, so she invested five dollars in a tabletop fryer. When a customer requested fried chicken, she was prepared. Her Louisiana family-style chicken was soon the talk of the town.

This Lincoln restaurant was a trendsetter. In the 1950s, it was one of the first Lincoln restaurants to show sports on television and to have air-conditioning. Jan (and formerly Ozzie) Wilcoxen have owned this iconic restaurant twice as long as the original owners.

ROCK ISLAND WRECK

Wilderness Park Area

On August 9, 1894, the train was trying to make up time to Fairbury. Unfortunately, the conductor did not know the trestle was about to crumble. As an act of evil intent, someone had taken apart the rails. Eleven died. Because of Henry Foote's bravery, even more survived. A historical marker is near the bike trail behind Southwest High.

WEST LINCOLN PARKS

Cushman Park was once located on West A Street. Borders blurred between several parks. With its boating, arcades, pool and merry-go-rounds, Electric Park was called the "Coney Island of the West." Named for its newfangled lights, the park offered picnics, vaudeville shows and even big animal acts.

South of town, a restaurant and hotel were named Lincoln Park. This spacious area included a theater and dance hall. At this location, one of Lincoln's most important movements began.

Since Lincoln Park Falls no longer exists, determining this exact location was challenging. It was possibly part of a dam but was definitely near Salt Creek. *Postcard from author's collection.*

EPWORTH LEAGUE

Inspired by New York's Chautauqua meetings, Lincoln Methodists planned summer gatherings. For the first five years, Lincoln Park became the "amen corner" of the city. Then the Epworth League purchased the nearby wooded area, and park development was underway.

The pavilion seated five thousand people. Especially on Venetian nights, decorated boats and rented canoes filled the lake. Nearby hotels and cabins were filled. Tickets could be purchased for the two-week sessions and were available to purchase every day but Sunday. At the end of the evening, twenty-five trolleys lined up to take attendees back to Lincoln. During the early years, thousands attended.

Besides religious subjects, speakers shared a variety of subjects, including attitude, success and current issues like Prohibition and prison reform. Early speakers hoped to get the "Chautauqua salute"—the crowd waving handkerchiefs in the air. Humorists entertained the crowd. Amateur and professional theater productions amused.

Some assembly speakers were well known. The local and favorite national Chautauqua speaker was William Jennings Bryan. From atop the pulpit, Billy Sunday's speech was fervent. At the conclusion of Booker T.

Located near First and Calvert, these gates once led to the Methodist's Epworth Park, where thousands used to gather for summer meetings. Today, they are found in Wilderness Park. *Photo by the author.*

Washington's first appearance, the audience felt so connected to his story that hundreds lined up to shake his hand. On Carrie Nation Day, she talked against everything from liquor to corsets to impolite Nebraska children. She even managed to sell some souvenir hatchets.

Due to the automobile and radio, attendance started declining. Nebraska Wesleyan students and other locals started joining the program. But what eventually ended Epworth Park was the rain. Several summer floods washed away the buildings. Today, the area is part of Wilderness Park.

PIONEERS PARK

3201 South Coddington Avenue

John Harris gave Lincoln quite the gift in 1928. In honor of his parents, he donated six hundred acres of southwestern land to nearby Lincoln. He chose the name to honor all who forged the state.

The Buffalo

For an opening piece, John Harris commissioned Paris sculptor George Gaudet to create a buffalo. After a rough ride at sea, the crate was lost. Lincoln did not offer a reward but was relieved when the statue arrived in the capital.

Near the end of its journey to the park, the statue's massive girth almost broke the Haynes Creek Bridge. Celebrating the successful crossing would have been fine if the truck's stop had not been on the railroad tracks. When he heard the whistle, the driver barely rumbled across in time.

Many Lincoln officials were there to see the first glimpse of the statue. After two hours of unloading, the buffalo was on its stand. Then the rain poured, and only two commissioners saw the unveiling.

Park Grounds

Ernst Herminghaus, Harvard landscape architect graduate, created the park's master landscape plan. His designs changed Lincoln. Not only did he beautify neighborhoods and parks, but he also was one of eight to pioneer the Lincoln Symphony.

The park was planted during the Dust Bowl years. Near the golf course, a reservoir helped with both flooding and drought control. Golf greens stayed vibrant. Designed by national golf course architect William Tucker, at first, Pioneers was a rare twenty-seven-hole course.

Lack of funds due to the Depression and World War II delayed Pinewood Bowl's construction until 1947. Herminghaus recognized that this particular hillside created a natural amphitheater. This is Lincoln's living World War II Memorial. Many enjoy attending the outdoor concerts and plays.

Later, the Chet Ager Nature Center was opened. As Lincoln Parks superintendent, Ager was responsible for getting the park going. Today, the zoo contains primarily native Nebraska animals and wildlife.

Park Pieces of the Past

On a park hill, a thirteen-foot-high Chief Red Cloud faces his former southwest tribe. With a fire at his feet, his blanket is about to be raised for the signal. This iconic *Smoke Signal* statue was designed by Ellis Luis Burman. To receive Works Progress Administration funding, the park department provided materials and Burman's lodging. Visitors today can still hike right up to the statue.

Williams Jennings Bryan gave his visiting friend Cotter McBride a Lincoln tour. Cotter thought the O Street Antelope Park entrance was lackluster. So, he gave Lincoln several thirty-two-foot drum columns purchased after the U.S. Treasury Building remodeling. The metal of the memorial plaque was salvaged from the battleship *Maine*. To limit the patrol area, part of Antelope Park was sold for 1950s commercial development. Both the columns and plaque were stored until the bicentennial celebration, when they were set near a Pioneers Park pond.

The next two buildings relocated to Pioneers Park when the Nebraska state fairgrounds moved out of Lincoln. Heritage School is a 1930s reproduction of Saunders County District 113 schoolhouse. If not for remodeling, Hudson Cabin may have stayed hidden.

In 1964, the Gullands were updating the 2236 South Ninth Street house they had purchased for her parents. When removing the woodwork between the living room and kitchen, they discovered logs hidden behind the plaster and lathe. A complete cabin was gradually uncovered.

Thomas Jefferson Hudson built this "prairie mansion" using logs from nearby Garland. As most early houses were dugouts or "soddies," having a shingled roof was elaborate. Hudson and his family had moved to Lancaster with Elder Young. Along with one other boy, their three kids completed the

Above: At first there was a gate around the Pioneers Park's buffalo to protect the statue from climbing children. *Photo by the author.*

Left: For the 1935 dedication of Burman's *Smoke Signal*, members of the Omaha, Ponca, Sioux and Winnebago tribes were part of the ceremony. *Photo by the author.*

When Abraham Lincoln addressed his Union soldiers in front of the U.S. Treasury Building, these pillars were still part of that building. *Photo by the author.*

Hudson Cabin—one of Lincoln's oldest buildings—was once covered up by another house. *Photo by the author.*

first Lincoln Sunday school. Hudson sold the cabin to Frank Sheldon in 1885. At some point, the cabin was concealed.

To save the cabin, Mayor Dean Peterson and his wife purchased the property. She relocated the cabin, as Ninth Street would not allow sightseeing. Turning the cabin into a Lincoln visitor's center at Van Dorn Park was considered. Ultimately, the city deeded the property to the Jaycees. Many contributed toward the restoration. The Hudson Cabin has now had three different Lincoln addresses.

8

A TO Z STREETS

I rather admire a town courageous enough to name its main street, "Zero Street."
—*Allen Ginsberg*

For a long time, Lincoln's O Street was considered the longest main street in the world. Outside of the downtown area, Lincoln rounded out as the streets were filled from A to Z.

EAST LINCOLN BAPTIST CHURCH (NOW THE MEETING PLACE)
2845 South Street

Constructed out of concrete blocks, this 1907 building was innovative. When the church closed in 1962, two other churches used the building. For almost thirty years, the Meeting Place has offered space to more than forty recovery groups, including Alcoholics Anonymous.

TEMPLE BAPTIST CHURCH
4940 Randolph Street

Due to moves and mergers, the history of Temple Baptist Church is hard to pinpoint. When the 1916 Calvary Baptist/Holdrege Baptist Church ended up next door to the 1908 Rush Baptist Mission Church, they shared a pastor.

Combining the congregations made sense. January 2, 1921, was the official opening of Temple Baptist.

This new congregation reconfigured a building. While under construction, headlights were used to light several evening services. Many pastors served during the first decade.

Throughout the Great Depression, money was unavailable to pay a pastor. Supply pastors, often only paid with food or gas money, kept Temple Baptist going. Families brought their own coal to light the furnace. To raise money, the church had a state fair booth. Ice cream socials were also popular.

In 1941, a pastor was hired for fifteen dollars per week. He lived in the church apartment and also acted as custodian. Soon, the church space needed to expand. The congregation paid what it could on the current mortgage, and the church conference helped with the rest.

For the new Forty-Ninth and Randolph building, church men donated labor and materials. During construction, they met at the Twenty-Seventh and Vine fire house. Through the years, as it continued to expand, God continued to provide. Darwin Penrod was one of the men in the middle who had a vision to keep the church going. He oversaw the additions. Today, his grandson Jeremy is the pastor.

HOLY TRINITY EPISCOPAL CHURCH
6001 A Street

Until the Nebraska bishop approved the building request, Episcopal services were held around the city. May 10, 1869, marked the beginning of the Church of the Holy Trinity. The state gave it three lots at Twelfth and J, and it spent $4,000 on the first building. At this location, the congregation constructed a Gothic red sandstone sanctuary in 1888. This would be its home for sixty-eight years. Through the years, many rectors led this downtown congregation.

In 1957, the beautiful downtown building burned to the ground. Many discussions happened next about whether this was still the best location for the church. By vote, they decided to move. Now, Lincoln Mall is at the former location. In front, a giant planter features a historic postcard reproduction that shows the former church.

Easter was the first official event before the May 1960 dedication. Two items were saved from the fire. Both the cross at the front of the altar and the sign near the columbarium are visual signs of God's faithfulness.

To design the sanctuary stained-glass windows, UNL art professor David Seyler traveled to Italy to learn glass making. His original crayon drawings are framed in the church's basement. His themes relate to the trinity. Windows were added as money was available. In the chancel bay, the five panels relate to church history and include the fire. Some figure sketches were based on church members. These windows demonstrate rebirth.

UNITARIANS

6300 A Street

In 1870, like-minded liberals joined to start the Universalist Society. On their three state lots at Thirteen and H, they built a frame building. Over twenty years later, a large brick building replaced it. In 1898, the church became Unitarian. This mix between a merger and a fresh start resulted in the All Souls Unitarian Church.

This building had an auditorium and dining area for square dancing. Two stained-glass windows were in the front. One honored the life of Mary Monell, who was influential in starting Lincoln's Universalist Society. Also in front was a beloved mural by Elizabeth Dolan, titled *In Search of Truth*. For her models, she used two young people, including her niece Margaret Cannell, who were a part of the congregation. When the church moved, the stained-glass window went along with it, but this mural went to the Cannells.

While the 1892 building was aging, the longtime janitor's retirement might have forced their relocation. "Old Gust" Johnson lived in the basement, did general repairs and kept the furnace going. As he was Lutheran, he did not attend services but spent most of his life in the dark downstairs. When he moved out, the church realized few would want to take that position. Updates only helped in the short-term.

In May 1957, the east Lincoln building tract was surrounded by cornfields. Within a decade, Taylor Meadows built around it. Today, this organization thrives on social action. It is also proud to bring together concepts from the world's religions and science.

FIRST LUTHERAN CHURCH
1551 South 70th Street

Thirteen singles and one couple were the Swedish Evangelical Lutheran Church charter members in 1870. Services were held in Swedish. Circuit-riding preachers filled the pulpit. Woodcarver Lars Sundean kept the church going with his sincere leadership and willingness to help.

The congregation took a step of faith and built on its three state lots. Sadly, the man in charge of the project mismanaged the money—$1,000 had been gathered, but workmen were not being paid. That same amount was still owed. To satisfy debts, one corner lot was sold. Years later, many still regretted that decision.

Members arrived in Lincoln from the East and from Sweden. Because these Swedes were often farmers, they stayed briefly in town before homesteading. This challenged church growth. Those who stayed struggled to support the church. Not until 1886 did the church have its first official pastor. Groundbreaking for its bigger church and parsonage happened on Reformation Day that year.

After building twice at Thirteenth and K, the members voted in 1932 to move into the former First-Plymouth Congregational Church at Seventeenth and A. At this point, only some of the services were in Swedish. The church started to be known as First Lutheran.

Through the years, the church has had many beloved pastors. On June 26, 1942, they gathered to celebrate Reverend Elliot and his wife's fortieth wedding and ministry anniversaries. Sadly, he passed away later that night. Through tragedy and triumph, this church united.

At the church's fiftieth anniversary, members wondered why no one had gone on to become a pastor. Their prayers for ministers were answered in due time. First Lutheran Church has now sent numerous sons and daughters into ministry across the United States and the world.

With several nearby Lutheran churches, First Lutheran decided to relocate to Lincoln's eastern edge. Its architectural inspiration was the Swedish stave church. Today, the church's sanctuary ceiling is still supported by timber framing. Both previous cornerstones became part of the new building. Since 1966, the church has served the community at this location.

Recently, the church decided the facility must be more accessible to match its welcoming statement. When the remodeling project is complete, the congregation plans to add a historical piece. In front of the former sanctuary, the *Christ in Gethsemane* stained-glass window has been stored since the move. Soon, this window will once again welcome all who enter.

WYUKA CEMETERY

3600 O Street

On fames eternal camping grounds
Their silent tents are spread.
—*Wyuka War veteran statue base*

Lincoln's original cemetery at Seventh and G became a "public nuisance" with repeated flooding. A few miles east of Lincoln, forty acres were set aside for a state cemetery. *Wyuka*, a common Nebraska cemetery name, means "place of rest" in Sioux.

By 1900, the cemetery had grown to almost 150 acres. Through the decades, one thousand Civil War veterans, many Nebraska governors and Lincoln leaders and more than fifty thousand citizens have been buried at this now-central location. Brick avenues curve around the gravestones. Lining O Street is the 1912 iron fence that once surrounded the university. The Wyuka Driving and Walking Tour is recommended to understand this historic site.

At Wyuka Cemetery, the lower Soldiers Circles is the resting place for those who served after the Civil War. On patriotic holidays, flags often adorn the individual gravesites. *Photo by the author.*

Potters Field was designated for state burials. Veterans are honored in the Soldiers Circles. For earlier conflicts, including the Civil War, a small oval of gravestones is found in the G.A.R. section. A civil war soldier stands guard. Former governor Thayer, colonel of the First Nebraska Territory Volunteer Infantry, is also recognized. Soldiers who fought in later conflicts are found in the larger, lower circle. Mount Lebanon is set aside for Reformed Jews.

During Lincoln's earlier days, citizens would picnic on the grounds due to its park-like setting. Today, visitors can again stroll across the historic bridge and feed the swans. Designed to hold caskets during winter, the 1886 receiving vault is still standing. Near the entrance, the 1910 stable has been repurposed for events. The 1936 Rudge Chapel still holds funerals and small weddings.

ANTELOPE GROCERY
2416 J Street

This Tudor Revival–style building combined commercial and residential elements. As the stained-glass sign still announces, the grocery store was on the main level. The original owners, Roy and Julia Palin, lived above in one "Leroy" apartment and rented the others. Today, this location has the same mixed usage.

PACE-WOODS HOUSE
2545 N Street

In 1886, the Pace family built this house. When their daughter, Clarke, married Mark Woods, the new couple moved there instead. Today, this location is home to Voices of Hope. This local organization provides support for abuse/assault victims and survivors to help them deal with trauma.

This large power plant building once pumped the city water and supplied electricity to city lights. *Photo by the author.*

A STREET POWER AND WATER STATION

2901 A Street

Located on a busy street due to energy demands, this station needed high style. The amount of electricity increased thirty-six times, which allowed Lincoln to grow. Today, water is pumped from Ashland, and this building houses condominiums.

ANTELOPE PARK

30th and A Street

Several Lincoln citizens donated land for recreational purposes. Antelope Park is a direct result of their generosity. While the area no longer stretches to O Street, the corridor is still long and narrow.

Lesser-known families, the Freys and Faulkners, donated part of their land. In 1907, William Jennings Bryan gave away ten acres of his Fairview Farm. Two memorials are on this section.

The thirty-two-foot war memorial was created by sculptor Ellis Luis Burman with funds from the Works Progress Administration. Soldiers are included from four conflicts: the Revolutionary War, the Civil War, the Spanish-American War and World War I. At the top, the spirit of war and victory stands guard.

On July 4, 1950, the city celebrated freedom. After being displayed across the state for several months, the Liberty Bell reproduction was brought to Antelope Park. As a gift, France had cast fifty-three such bells to be spread across the United States.

A Lincoln banker, W.T. Auld, gave fifteen nearby acres. Auld Pavilion, which opened in 1917 for gatherings and dances, was also completed because of his generosity. Near the south parking lot entrance, the pillared gates were constructed in Auld's honor.

Philip Edinborough assisted in beautifying Lincoln. He had been trained by some of Britain's finest landscape artists. Before his arrival in Lincoln, he helped plan the Trans-Mississippi Exposition in Omaha. Edinborough

Burman's War Memorial is twenty-three feet high with the nine-foot statue of victory soaring above. This monument was installed in 1936. *Photo by the author.*

worked with Superintendent William Schroeder. Park spaces in Lincoln grew from thirty-five to seven hundred acres.

Along Antelope Creek, the City Tourist Park was open from 1920 to 1932. Run by the Lincoln Auto Club, this public campground offered tent camping for a quarter or cabins for seventy-five cents. This area became part of Capital Parkway and is also used by the public schools. During the summer, thousands gathered at Antelope Park to hear music. John Shildneck directed the Municipal Band for many years. Today, the bandshell is named in his honor.

SUNKEN GARDENS

27th Street and Capital Parkway

Treasure from trash is true, as a tract was transformed during the Great Depression. When the city had redirected Antelope Creek, a pit resulted, and it became a place for trash to collect. The Seacrests donated the property for the upper half of the gardens, and Sara and Henry Frey donated the lower space. According to the paper, two hundred men worked at least two days a week in 1931 to transform the corner. The park's floriculturist, Fred Goebel, along with his son, Henry, worked out the design with park commissioner Ernest Bair.

At first, the park was called the Rock Garden. Stones of various shapes and sizes define the waterfall and retaining walls. The Glacial Till rock was found around the county. When the garden was completed, over four hundred trees and shrubs adorned the grounds. Unfortunately, they were not suited for the terrain.

Starting in the 1950s, the garden has contained annuals. With vibrant colors and particular themes, these flowers complete the space. Every year, capable volunteers help with planting the annuals. In the spring, they "Wake up the Beds." In November, more help to "Put the Beds to Bed."

For nearly seventy years, *Rebecca at the Well* was seen near the bottom of the waterfall. Ellis Burman completed this Works Progress Administraion project. Due to deterioration, the statue had to be removed in 2004. A year later, Nebraska artist David Young created a similar replacement piece.

This column cap from the second capitol is now at the Sunken Gardens. *Photo by the author.*

27ᵀᴴ AND CAPITAL PARKWAY GARDENS

In 1905, the city purchased the Sager Tract east of Twenty-Seventh. Part of this property benefitted the water department. Part was used for grazing for the horses that pulled park lawnmowers.

Later, part of this section was used for gardens. Goebel's Gardens, first filled with roses, honored the park floriculturist. Starting in 1945, Ernst Herminghaus set aside space for educational experimenting to determine what roses fit with Lincoln's climate. In 1978, the bicentennial fountain was installed nearby with funds raised by the Retired Teachers Association. In 2008, the gardens were redesigned to be more accessible. Don Hamann, a local jeweler who loved roses, donated $108,000 toward the project.

MUNICIPAL ZOO/AGER PLAY CENTER/THE SECRET JUNGLE
1300 South 27th Street

Money was tight, but labor was available. Thanks to Works Progress Administration funds, Lincoln continued to grow even during the Great Depression. A year-round zoo seemed necessary. The Antelope Park Zoo started with a scattering of animals throughout the park. The few inside animals were in a small greenhouse with limited access. An aviary building would provide Lincoln with visitor opportunities.

City workers quarried the limestone out of Roca. Lumber was milled from dead trees cut down in city parks. The department's portable saw purchase was used often during this time of drought. A skylight brought the sunshine inside. Not only did the zoo have exotic fowl, but monkeys and bears also lived in cages around the room. Adding to the natural habitat was the ten-foot waterfall that cascaded into the pond.

African American art student Roswell Coger created murals above the cages. The larger mural showed the animals in Nebraska. Outside, the landscape hedges were designed by Ernst Herminghaus.

When it opened, the zoo was considered the best west of Chicago and Saint Louis. Winter visitors were estimated at one hundred thousand. For a few decades, many came to experience exotic nature indoors. The zoo was renamed Chet Ager Memorial Zoo after the park supervisor who gave so much to Lincoln.

Experts determined that Lincoln had too many zoos, so the municipal zoo closed. This building became a temporary part of the Lincoln Children's Zoo. But by 1983, the animals were all gone. The space was transformed into an indoor playground where children enjoyed climbing, sliding and riding around.

In 2019, the building came full circle. The former Chet Ager Building became the Lincoln Children Zoo's Secret Jungle. Inside, both animals and kids can play. Monkeys climb and swing inside cages, and right next to those glass enclosures, children slide and scramble on playground equipment.

LINCOLN CHILDREN'S ZOO

Our zoo will offer more contact between people and animals than any other zoo in the world.

—*Arnott Folsom*

To commemorate Lincoln's 1959 centennial, Antelope Zoo added an area for children. Local businessman and longtime scoutmaster Arnott Folsom headed the expansion committee. He spent his retirement devoted to the zoo. He oversaw the five years of fundraising, guided zookeepers, completed landscape projects and was even known to give tours.

On opening day, July 21, 1965, children's admission was a quarter, and adults paid twice that. The Walton Railway Station is gone. But many early zoo features are still around, including the Crooked House, Leo the trash-eating lion and the stegosaurus fountain turned sandbox.

In 1986, John Chapo became one of the youngest zoo directors in the nation. Since then, he has continued to fulfill Folsom's vision. Under his leadership, the zoo has expanded its animal offerings and is now open year-round.

Although "robbers" no longer lurk at Holdup Hollow, riding the half-mile ZO & O Railroad track is an important Lincoln Children's Zoo tradition. *Photo by the author.*

NEPTUNE FOUNTAIN

11th and J Streets (Base Now near Twenty-Seventh and A Streets)

D.L. Thompson, who sold his house for the first governor's mansion, also donated the Neptune Fountain to the city. Bronze and steel figures soared from the center of the pool. Installation at the center of an intersection proved to be a traffic hazard. In 1920, the fountain was relocated to Antelope Park Zoo to become a goldfish pond and then a wading pool. While the figures were sold to Japan for salvage, the base continued to act as an animal enclosure. Today, the former pool is in front of the Ager Building, where it displays artwork.

FORMER MUNICIPAL BATHHOUSE

23rd and N Streets

The 1919 Municipal Bathhouse was a welcome addition to Lincoln for several decades. To cool off, swimmers enjoyed the center fountain and diving board. During the offseason, a local theater group performed inside.

This location became a symbol for progress in the Lincoln civil rights movement. Thanks to the efforts of numerous citizens, including the McWilliamses, the pool was finally open to all. Baseball fields are at this site now, and the former municipal building is offices.

TUTTLE-SCHAUPP HOUSE

3008 O Street

District judge and university law professor Samuel Tuttle served on the board of regents from 1875 to 1880. He arrived in Lincoln in March 1867. He married Blancy three years later. She was known for her singing and was a Lincoln Woman's Club charter member. Adam and Emma Schaupp were in the coal business. Their daughter, Zora, was a childhood education researcher. This home is now operated as Good Things Gift Shop.

WOODS PARK

33rd and J Streets

Within two years of opening, Woods Pool spectators had seen the world's best swimmers. In 1966 and 1968, Lincoln hosted the Amateur Athletic Union National Outdoor Swimming and Diving Championships. Since the Mexico City Olympics were in 1968, the Lincoln event became a U.S. trials qualifier. Don Schollander, Cate Ball, Gary Hall Sr. and Mark Spitz all competed in Lincoln.

Called the "fastest water in the west," Woods Pool had a separate warmup pool and eight competitive lanes. Towering over the sixteen-foot deep end were two springboards and three platforms of varying heights. Many children tested their courage when asked to jump from that highest tower. Many still spend summers at Woods Pool, but the diving platforms are closed. The nearby tennis courts, one of Lincoln's first club-level programs, are next to the new indoor facility.

LEON'S

2200 Winthrop Road

We'll deliver your groceries, but we draw the line at doing your dishes.

Leon's Stop and Shop was a butcher's shop in 1933. A few years later, Mr. Adelson hired university student Sam Davidson to help part-time. During World War II, the store closed because both men were serving the country.

In 1952, Leon's moved to its current location. Remodeling doubled the size of the store. Stage Door Deli, which opened in 1956, was one

Leon's Grocery has been part of the Rathbone Village shopping center for several decades. *Photo by the author.*

of Lincoln's first grocery store delis. For a time, Leon's was Nebraska's highest-volume grocery store.

When Leon died, Sam continued ownership. Two other employees purchased the property in 1988. Leon's is still known for its butcher shop and for stocking everyday and specialty items. Community also matters. For years, the store has been a longtime sponsor of a football team for little people.

TABITHA
4720 Randolph Street

Reverend Heiner saw that Lincoln needed an orphanage in 1886. Four years later, his group expanded to serve the homeless and older populations too. By 1907, a nursing school was added to train others to care for the sick. Through the decades, more services started, including a Meals on Wheels program. Today, Tabitha offers services ranging from rehabilitative to hospice care.

DRUMSTICK (NOW McDONALDS)
Near 48th and R Streets

When R.E.M. arrived in Lincoln to perform a 1982 show, they expected a night club. Much to their surprise, the Drumstick was actually a fried chicken restaurant. Tim Lohmeier, son of the original owner, had musical connections. For several years, he lined up several big gigs, including Dwight Yokum and Joan Jet and the Black Hearts. Part of the fun was the surprise at the venue. After two decades of chicken and eight years of live music, it closed in 1987. Trying to do both businesses was no longer paying off.

NATIONAL MUSEUM OF ROLLER SKATING
7700 A Street (Now 4730 South Street)

Slip on your hat and twirling dress and then grab the arm of your suited man. For twenty cents, couples could be part of the roller-skating craze. Rinks were found in many towns across the country.

The Detroit Arena Gardens held the first national dance and figure skating championships in 1938. Lincoln hosted the 1962 championships. A year in advance, a Texas company made the 75,500-pound collapsible skating floor.

This authentic 1962 ticket is from when Lincoln first hosted the American Amateur Roller-Skating Championships. *Photo by the author.*

Held at Pershing Auditorium, the event's success has resulted in Lincoln hosting the event often. In 1968, the Roller-Skating Rink Operator's Association (RSROA) moved its headquarters to the capital.

On October 27, 1980, organization members voted to start a museum They wanted to collect and display items that would tell the story of roller-skating. Now the collection includes a wall of wheels, displays on skating fashion and memorabilia of skating sports.

Operated by Tom and Mary Boydston, the Lincoln Rink (1918 O Street) opened in 1936. Many came to skate from the air force base. In 1949, the rink moved to the state fairgrounds. The next central Lincoln location closed in 1959. Tom was president of the RSROA and helped with that portable floor for the championships.

Arena Skate World opened in early 1950 at 300 North Forty-Eighth. Before the rink switched to records and tapes, Dick Carol played live organ music. In 1968, the name changed to Skate Zone "to keep up with the times." This final Lincoln rink closed in 2017. The roller-skating museum houses a commemorative poster signed by the rink's last skaters.

K'S RESTAURANT/PIEDMONT BISTRO BY VENUE

1725 Cotner Boulevard

When Kay Brestel started working at Scott's Pancake Shoppe, she was promoted quickly. Soon, she purchased the restaurant. Her down-home theme was as welcoming as her homemade breads and soups. Her back dining area was called the "Simba Room." Hundreds of lions and artifacts were displayed.

In spring 1983, Kay was shocked when *Terms of Endearment* asked to film some scenes at her restaurant. The film went on to win several Oscars. Lincoln was starstruck, including Mayor Boosalis, who climbed on top of chairs to see the filming.

New owners took over in 1996. But they did not keep the restaurant going. Today, the neighborhood can again enjoy dining at this location at the Piedmont Bistro by Venue.

BANKER'S LIFE/AMERITAS
5900 O Street

Five businessmen started a local insurance company in 1887. Old Line Banker's Life was Lincoln's first insurance company. Despite moves and expansions, this company ran out of a room downtown. In the late 1950s, it bought land on the eastern edge of town. Aside from growing the company, this move aided Lincoln's development. Today, this company is known as Ameritas.

GATEWAY MALL
6100 O Street

Adding a new shopping center to eastern Lincoln brought out a lot of feelings. Some people were excited, some were skeptical, and many were worried that downtown would change forever. While that did prove to be true, this 1961 center expanded the suburbs.

The new mall offered free community events, including pony rides, square dances and movies. Even a preliminary Miss Teenage America competition was held here. While free parking is still available, the advertised free stargazing is not because of the city lights. Through the years, the mall has changed names and its large department stores.

CHI HEALTH SAINT ELIZABETH
1145 South Street/555 South 70th

By request of Bishop Bonacum, four Franciscan sisters transformed a residence into a hospital. This first 1889 location near Twelfth and South was considered to be in the country. Patients paid what they could, so fundraising was part of the mission. Extra buildings were constructed to reach more needs. A nurse training school was added. For thirty years, this was Lincoln's only hospital.

The modern Saint Elizabeth Community Health Center opened in 1970 in east Lincoln. This location has continued to grow. As for the former hospital, it became a city-run nursing home called Lancaster Manor.

VETERANS ADMINISTRATION HOSPITAL
600 South 70th Street

Lincoln Veterans Hospital opened right before Christmas in 1930. Eastern windows provided country views. From some distance, the hospital water tower and smokestack were visible. Patient rooms were not private. Food was straightforward. With special equipment, the water was distilled. To protect those outside the room, the X-ray lab was lined with lead. This hospital was considered the "last word in beauty, modernity and efficiency." Veterans still come to this Lincoln outpatient clinic.

HISTORICAL LEAVITT HOUSE

In 1911, Burt W. Leavitt built a large stone-faced block house, complete with French red tile roof, east of Lincoln. Leavitt farmed, and he and his wife, Faythe, taught at nearby Cotner College. Eight years after they built it, the house was sold to the Benjamin Davis family.

Built as a country home, the Leavitt House was used by the VA hospital chief surgeon for several decades. *Library of Congress.*

When the U.S. government bought the farm in 1929, the residence housed the acting chief surgeon. Many families lived here until the VA stopped providing housing in 1980. For over two decades, the house was empty. Vandals destroyed the interior.

Bruce and Maureen Stahr saw value in the empty shell. Over two days in February 2003, a hired company moved the house eleven miles. Now the house is again east of Lincoln. Restoring the house to period condition took four years. The Leavitt House is the pivotal part of Prairie Creek Inn. Aside from overnight accommodations, many weddings and celebrations have brought new life to this century-old home.

HILLCREST
9401 O Street

After the Lincoln Country Club relocated out of its southwest building, leaders tried to sell it to the Shriners. Rather than taking the offer, they decided to build their own club east of town. A large recreation area offered picnics, croquet and fishing. The six-sided shelter included three fireplaces.

When the golf course opened on March 31, 1929, more than $300,000 had been spent. That fall, an epic match was played on the course. The plane carrying French Open winner Horton Smith and British Open winner Walter Hagen landed on the ninth fairway. They challenged the two Lincoln Country Club golf pros, Shriner Charley Koontz and John Morris. The two locals lost the competition by only a handful of strokes.

The Shrine Temple subsidized the club. Members ate for free and only had to pay for golfing. Considering the shrine was statewide, many did not like supporting this Lincoln endeavor. When the money ran out, the group was forced to sell.

Due to a series of sales and financial maneuvers by locals, the club changed names and owners a few times. To keep the club going, free golf was offered to anyone who helped maintain and mow the greens.

Another impressive 1963 golf exhibition involved Arnold Palmer beating Gary Player by two strikes. Golf is still important at the club but so is the pool. Hillcrest members have a beautiful recreational facility east of town.

9

SCHOOLS

This is the unexpected chapter. During the research process for this book, it became apparent that many Lincoln school names reflect Lincoln history. These are some of the stories worth telling. Elementary and middle schools are arranged in chronological order under their current corresponding high schools. Most private schools are listed at the end. Some school buildings are included in previous chapters.

FIRST SCHOOLS

George Peck became the first district school teacher in the fall of 1867. Thirty-five students paid fifty cents a month to learn. A year later, the number had doubled. The original Lincoln High was located at Fifteenth and North Streets. At first, the building seemed too large, but soon it was filled to capacity. Not long after, a new high school was needed.

LINCOLN HIGH (LINKS)
15th and M Streets (1872–1914)
2229 J Street (1915–Present)

I have great devotion to and pride in Nebraska. I'm proud to be a Nebraskan....I'm proud of the education I received in Nebraska.
                    —*Ted Sorenson, 1942 Lincoln High graduate*

Walking into Lincoln High is like taking a step back into history. As Lincoln's oldest high school, students have been attending this location since 1913. Names engraved into the marble at the entrance attest to this. Students who sacrificed their lives for freedom are remembered, including World War I soldiers. The gray-veined white marble is from the same quarry as the Lincoln Memorial and the Tomb of the Unknown Soldier. Over sixty flags hang from the ceiling. These represent the cultures and countries that have been part of the school. Along with one other Nebraska school, Lincoln High participates in the International Baccalaureate Program.

At first, the school was on the edge of town. Parents were nervous about their students crossing Antelope Creek Bridge, so adjustments were made. Offering students lunch meant less time walking around town.

Early class options at this "Palace of Learning" included household arts and manual training. On the top floor, art was taught in sky-lit studios. At one time, the walls were a gallery. To allow students to go directly to teaching, normal training took place. The school pool seemed like a good idea, but due to leaking, the pool is now filled in and is underneath the school library.

While Lincoln High auditorium's seating is more comfortable today, the original wooden chairs allowed for a bigger crowd. *Photo by the author.*

From the beginning, the theater made history. In 1914, the opera performance featured the first cast made entirely of students west of the Allegheny. Today, the auditorium is known as Ted Sorensen Theatre. This 1945 alum is best known for being John F. Kennedy's speechwriter. He also assisted with Kennedy's 1957 Pulitzer Prize–winning book, *Profiles in Courage*. Other notable alumni include Dick Cavett and Sandy Dennis.

The Link's song, "Sons of the Black and Red," can be heard at school contests. Starting in 1891, Lincoln High fielded a football team. It often played the university during the early days. The Links have won many state championships.

THE FOLLOWING TWO SCHOOLS are closely connected. In 1992, Park and Everett traded students. Park became the middle school, and Everett reverted back to an elementary.

PARK MIDDLE SCHOOL (PANTHERS)
855 South 8th Street (1882–1925; 1926–Present)

Built next door to Lincoln's first park, this building has held kindergarten through eighth at various times. The attached community center once offered general Sunday school classes and a library. Mothers had their own club, and they could attend home nursing classes with their daughters. Game rooms were also popular.

EVERETT ELEMENTARY (EAGLES)
1123 C Street (1887–1928; 1928–Present)

Once called C Street School, the name was eventually changed to Everett. As a congressman, Massachusetts governor, England envoy, Harvard president and unsuccessful presidential candidate, Edward Everett was an excellent speaker and education champion. Everett started as an elementary school and then was Lincoln's third junior high in 1928.

CAPITOL SCHOOL 1886–1963

NOW McPHEE ELEMENTARY (MUSTANGS) 1965–PRESENT
820 Goodhue Boulevard

Clair McPhee was principal for forty-two years at this downtown school. During that time, students watched the demolition and reconstruction of the capitol. A new school was built and renamed McPhee. Clair is the only teacher who actually worked at the school named in her honor.

ELLIOT ELEMENTARY (OWLS)
26th and O Streets (1888–1922)
225 South 25th Street (1922–Present)

Phoebe Elliot was Lancaster County's first teacher at the log house (Old Sand Hill School) near Roca. Later, she moved to Lincoln. She joined the school board and became the first Lincoln Women's Club president in 1894.

Photographs from 1918 show Elliott Elementary students planting World War I victory gardens. Classrooms were encouraged to take garden breaks. The community grew its own vegetables in nearby lots. Still today, gardening classes are part of the Elliott Learning Community.

CHERRY
Twentieth and Cherry/Sumner Streets (1889–1922)
NOW PRESCOTT SCHOOL (PRIDE)
1930 South 20th Street (1922–Present)

Many south Lincoln streets were named for fruit. When a new school building opened in 1921, some parents did not want to rename Cherry for Prescott. William Hinkling Prescott wrote historical accounts, including the conquest of Mexico. For a long time, the school was still called "Cherry," even in the newspaper.

Starting in 1907, this school provided services for deaf children. It is known for its community gardens. Even more stories are linked on the school's website.

Prescott School's new 1922 building was designed by local architects Fiske and Meginnis. *Photo by the author.*

SARATOGA ELEMENTARY (STARS)

2215 South 13th Street (1893–Present)

Location determined the name of this school. Next to the street, Saratoga was probably named for a Revolutionary War battle. Through the years, Saratoga has undergone both additions and remodeling.

RANDOLPH ELEMENTARY (ROADRUNNERS)

27th and Randolph area (1899–1925)
1034 South Thirty-Seventh Street (1925–Present)

Lyman Frost's family owned farm grounds from Third to Fortieth Streets. In the middle of his farm, between F and I Streets, it crossed Randolph Street. This street is named for the Pocahontas descendent who became a Virginia statesman. In the upstairs, Frost's daughter taught eight students. Later, a school building was constructed on the property near Thirty-Third and Randolph. Until it was leveled by a tornado, Frost School became the community center. The replacement four-room schoolhouse was built in 1901 at Twenty-Sixth and Randolph. It is an American Legion Park today.

The middle of a cornfield at Thirty-Seventh and D Streets was chosen as the next school location in 1926. Nearby, the neighborhood pond was used for swimming and ice skating. Because of the creek and willow trees, the lower playground was restricted. Three additions have helped keep up with school population growth.

NUERNBERGER EDUCATION CENTER (NIGHTHAWKS)

1801 South 40th Street (2016–Present)

Students overwhelmed with traditional middle school are sent to the Nuernberger Education Center. Judge Bill Neurnberger fought for a youth court and then became the original Lancaster County Juvenile Court judge. Off the clock, he also devoted time to help children have better lives.

LINCOLN EAST HIGH (SPARTANS)

1000 South Seventieth Street (1967–Present)

Charge with your might. Fight for the blue and white. Lincoln East Spartans.
—"Spartan Fight Song" by Chuck Pennington and Jay Booster.

Schools were overflowing with students. Lincoln East opened in 1967 as a junior and senior high. The three interconnected wings allowed for a functional, modern school. For thirty years, it planned a "comprehensive academic curriculum" for a wide range of ages. Today, East is still full but only with senior high students.

During the turbulent '60s, some students planned a walkout and announced it to the media. When East's first principal found out, he pulled the fire alarm. Principal McGrew defused the situation, since a fire drill was not front-page news.

Students picked the mascot—Martin the Spartan. The bright blue and white from the Greek flag became the colors. The student newspaper is the *Oracle* and the yearbook is the *Epic*.

Through the years, the fierce Spartans have won numerous state sport titles. Donated by the longtime Lincoln family, Seacrest Field is where most Lincoln football games are played. Masters Weeks recognizes East graduates changing the world.

HAWTHORNE ELEMENTARY (1913–2008)

BRYAN COMMUNITY (PHOENIX) (1980–PRESENT)
300 South 48th Street

Named for author Nathaniel Hawthorne, this school was built on the east edge of town. The first building was replaced. Due to low enrollment, Hawthorne closed its doors to elementary students.

Down the street, Bryan Elementary School (named for William Jennings Bryan) served students from 1956 to 1971, when it was also closed. At first, the building was for storage, until it became an alternative high school. In 2011, the school relocated to become the Bryan Community Focus Program at Hawthorne

Bryan's quote, "Destiny is not a matter of chance, it is a matter of choice. It is not a thing to be waited for, it is a thing to be achieved," inspires staff and students to remember that choices matter. While previous decisions may have led the students to an alternative location, they can now choose to go in a different direction.

LUX MIDDLE (LIGHTNING)
7800 High Street (1996–Present)

A person's ideas, ideals, and institutions live on through the lives of the people they have touched.

—John Lux

After graduating from Northeast, John Lux went to Nebraska Wesleyan and then to UNL for graduate degrees. He became the UNL Teacher Corps director. Not only was he on the Lincoln Public Schools Board, but he also served with Huntington PTA on behalf of his kids. By combining innovation, mathematics and science, Lux developed techniques to help teachers improve the educational process.

MOORE MIDDLE (MOUNTAIN LIONS)

8700 Yankee Woods Drive (2017–Present)

On the day Moore Middle School opened, Dr. Marilyn Moore was there—not to give a speech but to spend time talking to seventh graders about the power of story. Moore started her teaching career at Goodrich Middle School and then spent decades serving students, including as an administrator with instruction policies. Outside of school, she helped Lincoln non-profit organizations.

As part of the partnership with the Copple Family YMCA next door, the two locations share gym spaces. Through the years, Ed Copple worked in banking and developed Lincoln neighborhoods. He and his wife received a 2012 award for their charitable contributions.

EASTRIDGE ELEMENTARY (EAGLES)

6245 L Street (1955–Present)

In 1954, the Eastridge neighborhood was on the edge of Lincoln. Because the building was not quite ready, five homes on Randolph Street housed the first students. The following year, the building opened.

MORLEY ELEMENTARY (MEADOWLARKS)

6800 Monterey Drive (1960–Present)

In 1900, Mrs. May Morley started teaching. Fifteen years later, she became Prescott's principal and stayed there for thirty-one years. Morley Elementary was once on the edge of town. In 2002, fourth grade teacher Renee Kovar wrote the school song with her disc jockey husband, Mick.

PYRTLE ELEMENTARY (PANTHERS)

721 Cottonwood Drive (1965–Present)

As one of the first Lexington High graduates, Ruth Pyrtle was always a trendsetter. While working for Lincoln Public Schools, she completed both undergrad and master's degrees at the university. She served as both McKinley High principal and Bancroft Elementary principal. She was once the National Education Association president and trained teachers.

HUMANN ELEMENTARY (HUSKIES)
6720 Rockwood Lane (1990–Present)

Julius Humann might have been a Renaissance man. He taught mathematics and music and retired to teach barbecue cooking. He started at College View and then became Northeast's assistant principal. Later, he worked in pupil personnel services.

When deciding the school nickname, many funny names were suggested to connect with "human." The school motto is "We're All Humann: Learn, Grow, Succeed."

MAXEY ELEMENTARY (MUSTANGS)
5200 South 75th Street (1995–Present)

JoAnn Maxey helped at the schools where her four children attended. She wanted schools to become more multicultural. She ran for the Lincoln School Board in 1975. Then she served two years as a state senator before returning to the school board. As the first African American in both positions, she understood what it was like to feel alone. Representing others, especially minorities, became her mission.

Since 1959, JoAnn and her high school sweetheart husband were part of Lincoln. He was one of the first African American basketball scholarship players at the university. Later, he served on the Lincoln Police Force for thirty-two years. She worked as Malone Senior Center manager and loved others well. When cancer took her life at age fifty-four, the Malone Center was renamed after her.

LINCOLN SOUTHWEST HIGH SCHOOL (SILVER HAWKS)
7001 South 14th Street (2002–Present)

Lincoln's growth went south. When these doors opened in 2002, seventy-seven teachers were ready for the 1,150 high schoolers. Block scheduling was a new approach. Due to its location next to Wilderness Park, the outdoor classroom is an important part of learning.

SCOTT MIDDLE SCHOOL (STARS)

2200 Pine Lake Road (1996–)

Eighteen-year-old Hazel Scott taught at South Bend Country School. Six years later, she moved to College View High School. Over time, she became assistant and then the first female principal. When College View closed, she moved to Southeast with her students to continue in administration until 1965. Sadly, she died the day before the announcement was made that Lincoln's next middle school would be named "Scott."

To connect with the community, Scott presents an annual award. The Martin Luther King Jr. Wall of Honor recognizes those who better Lincoln by being positive multicultural role models.

RUTH HILL ELEMENTARY (HAWKS)

5230 Tipperary Trail (1976–Present)

Hill Hatchery was founded and developed during the Great Depression. Ruth Hill helped her husband with the business, but she also wanted to make a difference by serving. For eighteen years, she served as the first woman on the Lincoln Public School Board. Although she retired to Arizona, when she returned, she always visited the 1976 school named for her.

CAVETT ELEMENTARY (CARDINALS)

7701 South 36th Street (1995–Present)

The Cavetts served Lincoln together. Along with her Lincoln Public Schools position, Doris taught mathematics on television and was a well-liked UNL teachers college professor. Her husband, Alva, taught at Lincoln High and handled the business side of its athletic department. When he retired, he took a similar management position at Seacrest Field for twenty years.

ROPER ELEMENTARY (ROCKETS)

2323 South Coddington Avenue (1995–Present)

In the early years, the Lincoln Police Department matrons served the community. But the first actual female officer was Hulda Roper. Starting in 1944, her role included helping families. Through the years, she started Opportunity Camp for disadvantaged youngsters and Cedars Home for Children. She also helped establish the juvenile court system. At Roper, an outdoor garden is maintained by the West A organization.

ADAMS ELEMENTARY (AVIATORS)
7401 Jacobs Creek Drive (2008–Present)

From Tuskegee fighter pilot to industrial arts teacher, Lieutenant Colonel Paul Adams lived a full life. While serving in World War II, he was part of nine key campaigns. For his service, he received the Commendation Medal with three oak leaf clusters. Next, Adams went to work for Lincoln Public Schools in 1964. He was one of only three African Americans teachers. For almost twenty years, he taught kids to work with their hands.

Although he retired, he continued to serve Lincoln. He was local NAACP president. As a part of Capital City Kiwanis, he started the East High Builders Club. For Elliott Elementary students, he became "Grandpa." He and his wife of sixty-seven years, Alda, were involved at their church.

POUND MIDDLE (SQUIRES—KNIGHTS IN TRAINING)
4740 South 45th Street (1963–Present)

The Pound family believed in education. Judge Stephen, an early Lincoln pioneer, made sure that his three children were educated, even on the plains. Roscoe had his doctorate at nineteen, became the university law dean and then went on to the same at Harvard. Louise, a notable athlete, taught foreign languages at the university.

Olivia impacted Lincoln Public Schools the most. For forty-three years, she was at Lincoln High. First, she taught Latin and then became the girls' advisor and assistant principal. Beyond the classroom, Olivia Pound was the author of almost twenty textbooks and numerous educational articles. She was National Association of University Women president for a time.

At first, Pound was a junior high. It was opened in 1963, when schools were reorganizing. Calvert sent seventh graders, and the eighth and ninth graders and many teachers came from Southeast. In 2003, the school became a sixth through eighth grade middle school.

COLLEGE VIEW SOUTH WARD (PIONEERS) (1929–38)

College View High (1929–55); College View Elementary (1929–58)

CALVERT ELEMENTARY (COYOTES)

3725/3709 South 46th Street

College View High started in 1892 and moved to a new location in 1920. Within a few years, 150 students were attending. This school had notable football players and won the 1945 class C basketball championship. The class of 1955 was the last purple and gold graduates.

In 1958, the elementary school was renamed Calvert after the street. Two College Views were too many. In the 1880s, T.E. Calvert lived in Lincoln and was the Burlington and Missouri River Railroad general superintendent and chief engineer.

Although Dick Cheney would move and become a Wyoming congressman, he attended this neighborhood school. Cheney became the forty-sixth U.S. vice president.

LINCOLN SOUTHEAST HIGH SCHOOL (KNIGHTS)

2930 South 37th Street (1956–Present)

Over seventy people planned the new Southeast High School. Until Pound junior high opened, seventh through twelfth grade students attended. Fifty-eight students graduated in 1956. Over five hundred seniors graduate now.

To develop school spirit, students had an emblem contest. Above the chosen shield is a knight's head. On the shield are the letters "S" and "E," along with six owls in honor of the original grades.

Through the years, this school has won more than one hundred state championships. Two graduates, Robert J. Hibbs and Charles C. Hagemeister, won Congressional Medals of Honor for their military service. More Southeast graduates have attended UNL than any other school.

In the auditorium, the 1976 *Investment* mural by Seward professor Reinhold Marxhausen still inspires students today. All shapes and lines are formed of wood, ceramic, Formica and metal. His concept features the progression of going from black to gold. Various stages of seeds imply growth and reaching potential.

HOLMES ELEMENTARY (HEDGEHOGS)

5230 Sumner Street (1937–Present)

George Holmes became president of First National Bank. He asked that land he donated for a school be named after his mother, Emma Holmes, who was an early Lincoln settler. The building was constructed at the site of the family's former farmhouse and barn.

SHERIDAN ELEMENTARY (SHARKS)

3100 Plymouth Avenue (1926–Present)

Along Sheridan Boulevard are many of the city's early fine homes. The nearby boulevard and school were named for Union Civil War general Phillip Henry Sheridan. Surrounding this school, the purple flowers reflect an early Lincoln nickname, the "Lilac City."

ROUSSEAU ELEMENTARY SCHOOL (RAMS)

3701 South 33rd Street (1964–Present)

Miss Maude Rousseau started with Lincoln Public Schools in 1918. She taught at Elliot and then went to Whittier where she was girls' advisor and assistant principal. For twenty-one years, she was the first Randolph principal.

BEATTIE ELEMENTARY (BOBCATS)

1901 Calvert Street (1953–Present)

Merle Beattie became a teacher at age twenty-one. For the next forty-five years, she served the district. From 1923 to 1951, her position was director of elementary education.

IRVING MIDDLE SCHOOL (AARDVARKS)

2745 South 22nd Street (1927–Present)

Built in 1927, Irving Middle School shares the building with the Irving Recreation Center. Washington Irving wrote classics, including *Rip Van Winkle* and *Legend of Sleepy Hollow*. Irving School has had long-term principals.

Irving is home to the Chimney Swift Club. Due to the steam rising from their large brick chimney, the cylinder has become a nesting colony for certain South American birds. During the warmer months, the swifts swoop high in the air while hunting for insects. Video cameras let students witness these "flying cigars" birds firsthand.

LEFLER MIDDLE SCHOOL (LIONS)
1100 South 48th Street (1955–Present)

Millard Lefler was a Lincoln High assistant principal starting in 1917. His next administration title was superintendent of measurements and research. Then he was selected to be the Lincoln Public Schools superintendent from 1920 to 1948. His time of service went from the Roaring Twenties until after World War II.

Lefler transitioned Lincoln into the junior high system. He also supported the start of both vocational training and adult education. Though money was scarce, he budgeted for new schools. His contributions were invaluable.

After retirement, he went to Japan to become an educational consultant at General MacArthur's headquarters. For his next career, he became a Lincoln real estate agent. He lived to be ninety-four.

ZEMAN ELEMENTARY (ZEBRAS)
4900 South 52nd Street (1974–Present)

For forty years, Anna Zeman served Lincoln Public Schools. Until 1946, she taught at Clinton and was Havelock's assistant principal. For the last twenty years, she was principal at Calvert Elementary School.

WYSONG ELEMENTARY (WOLVES)
7901 Blanchard Avenue (2016–Present)

Beyond simply teaching children, Sally Wysong wanted to change their lives. For thirty-one years, she directed Meadowlane Nursery School. In her off hours, she was part of numerous educational committees, including the Lincoln Public School Board. Her "enthusiasm and expertise" benefitted and bettered the lives of many children.

KLOEFKORN ELEMENTARY (CUBS)
6601 Glass Ridge Drive (2012–Present)

Not many things are more important or more satisfying than classrooms filled with wide-eyed, vibrant students who are eager to learn and to tell stories by way of the written word.

—*William Kloefkorn*

This Nebraska writer published many collections of poetry, but William Kloefkorn was a teacher at heart. He was a Nebraska Wesleyan writing and literature professor for over forty years. To connect students to poetry, he developed the Poets in the Schools program. He presented workshops and connected with learners across Nebraska and the United States. As a friendly former football player with a deep voice, he commanded attention.

LINCOLN NORTHEAST HIGH (ROCKETS)
2635 North 63rd Street (1941–Present)

Trying to unify three rival schools (Havelock, Jackson from University Place and Bethany) at one location was challenging. Even picking a name was hard. Many wanted to name the school for a person, like Pershing, not for a direction. The next issue was the nickname. At first, teams were called the HUB in honor of the former three schools. Students preferred Rockets, Raiders or Pirates. Because of the Rock Island Rocket train, Rockets was chosen.

The Ed Johnson gym honors the Northeast coach who had eight basketball championships. The band played at the 1994 Rose Bowl game. Notable alumni include Nebraska politician Bob Kerry, Nebraska governor, senator and presidential candidate. Once a longtime legislator, alum Don Wesley later served as mayor. Graduate Tom Casady became Lincoln police chief.

In the 1990s, the school's symbol, a large silver rocket, disappeared. In honor of the school's seventy-fifth anniversary, a campaign was started to "raise the rocket" again. Facing northeast, the new rocket is three-sided to represent the three communities that came together to create the school.

HARTLEY ELEMENTARY (HORNETS)
730 North 33rd Street (1921–Present)

Ellis T. Hartley started in Ohio, but in the 1880s, along with his wife, he relocated to Lincoln. From 1883 to 1890, he served as Lincoln Public Schools superintendent. At that point, he chose farming instead. Until his death in 1914, he planted fruit trees on his land. No one wanted the orchard, so the land was later sold off.

CULLER MIDDLE (COUGARS)
5201 Vine Street (1958–Present)

Charles Culler was a draftsman teacher and then Lincoln High assistant principal. But for twenty-six years, he was the Whittier Junior High School principal. Culler served Lincoln well in the educational field. Although the Cullers did not have children, Charles invested in community, especially in Boy Scouts. For five years, this location was also an elementary school before it only served the middle grades.

MICKLE MIDDLE (MISSILES)
2500 North 67th Street (1960–Present)

Robin Mickle started his career at Jackson High. When Northeast opened, he moved with the students to become the counselor. In 1945, he became principal and stayed there until he died in 1957. Because most students become Northeast Rockets, the Mickle mascot is the Missile. This school was one of the first in Lincoln to switch from the junior high model to middle school in 1993.

JACKSON HIGH (1912–41)

HUNTINGTON ELEMENTARY (EAGLES) (1912–1927)
4601 Adams/2900 North Forty-Sixth Street

This was the University Place school corner. Eleven students attended that first year in the wooden schoolhouse. Two boys were the first graduates in 1895. The school built a new brick building in 1911 because over two hundred students were attending.

When University Place became part of Lincoln, the school needed a new name. William Robert Jackson had been Wesleyan's Teacher College dean and on the school board. Known for academics and athletics, Principal Robin Mickle and his assistant principal Mable Thompson led well. Many cheered on notable coach Beechner's Cardinal football team.

During the 1920s and 1930s, this was one of Nebraska's largest high schools. In 1941, the school closed. Students went to Northeast. Jackson High was remembered with reunions.

Huntington Elementary School was built next door in 1921. W.C. Huntington had been a Trinity Methodist Church minister until he became Wesleyan chancellor. In 1997, students attended school at the Nebraska fairgrounds while a new building was constructed to replace the old one.

FORMER BENTON ELEMENTARY
49th and Benton Street (1955–57)

DAWES MIDDLE (DIAMONDBACKS) (1957–2009; 2011–PRESENT)
5130 Colfax Avenue

When Charles Dawes left Lincoln after seven years, he went on to be a negotiator, a vice president and an ambassador. Dawes Middle School operated as both an elementary and junior high. In 1991, the younger kids moved elsewhere. Dawes temporarily closed due to low enrollment, so students attended "Goodrich at Dawes" here from 2009 to 2011. That fall, Dawes reopened again.

CLINTON ELEMENTARY (COMETS)
1520 North Twenty-Ninth (1891–Present)

DeWitt Clinton was a New York governor in 1825, who stood for democracy and helped organize the Erie Canal. Located near Twenty-Seventh Street by the Rock Island Railroad tracks, the school consisted of one room. In 1891, Clinton opened at its current location, but that building was replaced with a Gothic one in 1925.

RILEY ELEMENTARY (RAMS)

5051 Dudley (1910–63)

5021 Orchard Street (1964–Present)

When life was like a story, holding neither sob nor sigh,
In the golden olden glory of the days gone by.

—*James Whitcomb Riley*

Poems like these gave James Whitcomb Riley the nickname the "Children's Poet." During its early years, this 1892 white frame building was simply called Ward 3. One hundred students crammed into two rooms. In 1913, a larger brick building was added to the campus. At that point, Riley Elementary came into being. When University Place became part of Lincoln, so did this school.

On March 10, 1964, the students left for lunch. Soon after, someone noticed smoke, and the custodian found a fire. All materials, band instruments and clothing left behind were ruined. But the children were safe. The school was rebuilt next door. For almost forty years, this original school stayed standing. In 2001, developers sold lots at the old school site. The students watched as the century-old building was disassembled.

NORWOOD PARK ELEMENTARY (ROADRUNNERS)

4710 North 72nd Street (1921–Present)

The school name came from a nearby area called North Woods. A 1958 addition and remodeling has kept the building updated. The school newsletter is the *Beep*.

PERSHING ELEMENTARY (COMETS)

6402 Judson Street (1955–Present)

Although he rarely returned, General John Pershing considered Lincoln his town. The capital city gladly adopted this notable man. At the nearby YMCA, afterschool clubs include crafts, cooking, running and more.

MEADOW LANE ELEMENTARY (MUSTANGS)
7200 Vine Street (1955–Present)

Meadow Lane neighborhood needed a school. Ten area houses were purchased and used for classrooms for two years until the building was ready. It later added more classrooms and a bigger library.

BROWNELL ELEMENTARY (BUFFALOES)
6000 Aylesworth Avenue (1958–Present)

Herbert and May Brownell loved children. Mrs. Herbert, as she was known, was 1949 Nebraska Mother of the Year. She shared her wisdom in various columns. Hebert was an education professor at different universities and wrote textbooks.

Education was so important to the family that five of the seven children became teachers. Three daughters even married professors. Herbert Jr. was Dwight D. Eisenhower's attorney general. Samuel was a Yale professor and a U.S. commissioner of education.

KAHOA ELEMENTARY (COUGARS)
7700 Leighton Avenue (1972–Present)

Evelyn Kahoa taught and was principal at multiple schools throughout her forty-year career. For five years, she was principal of both Bethany and Riley at the same time. Students remember her fondly.

NORTH STAR HIGH SCHOOL (NAVI-GATORS)
5801 North 33rd Street (2003–Present)

Opening in 2003, students picked the name because of what the north star represents. Through the years, this night wonder has guided people to their destinations.

GOODRICH MIDDLE (DRAGONS)

4600 Lewis Avenue (1969–Present)

Thomas Goodrich was a Lincoln High teacher when he married Principal Emma Morrell from Everett. She stayed at her position until her 1936 retirement. Thomas supervised the vocational program and then joined Lincoln Public School administration as director of measurement and research.

Many wanted to honor both Goodriches with the school name. But on paper, the board named the school after him. During the 2009 through 2011 remodeling, it was known as "Goodrich at Dawes Middle School."

SCHOO MIDDLE (SKYHAWKS)

700 Penrose Drive (2009–Present)

For almost twenty years, Dr. Philip Schoo was Lincoln Public Schools superintendent. Throughout his tenure, he was known for empowering his team and for working hard. To find his thoughts on the value of middle schoolers, visit the Schoo website. Since Schoo shares building space with the Fallbrook YMCA, students have additional opportunities.

WEST LINCOLN ELEMENTARY (WILDCATS)

630 West Dawes Avenue (1886–Present)

West Lincoln was its own town. Starting in 1886, school was in session. Through the years, the number of students grew. As for the teachers, their responsibilities grew, but due to financial depressions, their pay sometimes decreased. On the school website, the history is well documented.

In 1965, West Lincoln School was annexed into Lincoln. Seventh grade students were bussed into the city. A mural in the media center shows the original schoolhouse.

BELMONT ELEMENTARY (COUGARS)

12th and Belmont Streets (1889–1922)
3425 North 14th Street (1922–Present)

When this suburb started, there were eighteen Belmonts across the United States. The first two-story school had four rooms. By 1921, the relocation helped with growth. Through the years, school expansions included a community center.

LAKEVIEW ELEMENTARY (SEAGULLS)

300 Capitol Beach Boulevard (1913–Present)

Lakeview started as a one-teacher school. When an expansion was needed, the teachers built the school—literally. They felt that their abilities matched the skills of other carpenters and were allowed to prove their point. Student numbers were lower until 1945, when the area developed.

FREDSTROM ELEMENTARY (FALCONS)

5700 Northwest 10th Street (1983–Present)

Home, school, church and community are the fundamental building blocks of American Society. Only to the extent that these four institutions work together will there be effective education and a forward moving society.
—Rudolph L. Fredstrom

As "most versatile" Midlands College student, this phrase would define Fredstrom's life. From teacher/coach to Nebraska Wesleyan education director to Lincoln Public Schools student services department member, he impacted education. When Fredstrom visited the school named for him, he emphasized to students to "never stop learning."

CAMPBELL ELEMENTARY (COYOTES)
2200 Dodge Street (1995–Present)

Dr. Anne Campbell served many roles in the education world. She was a school superintendent, program director and UNL public affairs director. As state education commissioner, she also helped with the notable report "A Nation at Risk."

KOOSER ELEMENTARY (KODIAKS)
7301 North 13th Street (2009–Present)

The thirteenth poet laureate of the United States was once an insurance vice president. Ted Kooser made his living at Lincoln Benefit Life, but writing made his life. He has received multiple awards, including a Pulitzer in 2005. As a part of the new elementary, the grounds include a small park.

ARNOLD ELEMENTARY SCHOOL (EAGLES)
5000 Mike Scholl Street (1959–2008; New Building 2009–Present)

Not only did General Henry "Hap" Arnold command the United States Army Air Corps in World War II, but he is also one of only nine five-star generals in the United States. As the "Father of the Modern Air Force," several books have been written about his achievements. But he was also a writer. Some of his children adventure chapter books about flying are still available.

Although federal funds constructed the school, it has always been a part of Lincoln Public Schools. The school closed with the air force base but then reopened a year later. Since the Lincoln Housing Authority bought the base houses, plenty of students have moved into the neighborhood. Attached to the new 2009 building is a shared library that is open after hours to the public.

LINCOLN PIUS X HIGH SCHOOL (THUNDERBOLTS)
6000 A Street (1956–Present)

Street Theresa's, or Cathedral High, was the first Catholic high school in Lincoln. But the Lincoln Catholic Diocese bishop Bonacum and other local leaders wanted a Catholic high school in the middle of town. The Great Depression delayed the plans.

Fifty-three students were part of the 1957 graduating class from Piux X. Today, over three hundred students graduate per year. The Bolts excel in both athletics and academics. Aldrich Field pays tribute to Coach Vince, who was part of many football victories.

Since schools reflect their parish names, they are often named for saints. Recently, Saint Mary's and Sacred Heart Schools closed and joined other elementary schools. Lincoln Catholic schools include:

Saint Mary's; 1434 K Street (1960–2018)
Saint Patrick; 4142 North Sixty-First Street (1916–present)
Blessed Sacrament; 1725 Lake Street (1926–present)
Sacred Heart; 3128 South Street (1928–2019)
Saint Teresa; 616 South Thirty-Sixth Street (1930–present)
Cathedral of the Risen Christ; 3245 South Thirty-Seventh Street (1954–present)
Saint John's; 7601 Vine Street (1954–present)
Saint Joseph; 1940 South Seventy-Seventh Street (1979–present)
Saint Peter's; 4500 Duxhall Drive (1991–present)
North American Martyrs; 1101 Isaac Drive (1996–present)
Saint Michael's; 9101 South Seventy-Eighth Street (2011–present)

LINCOLN LUTHERAN (WARRIORS)
1100 North 56th Street (1995–Present)

In the 1950s, the Lincoln Lutheran School Association was organized. Calvary and Trinity already had K-8 schools, but they were crowded. Starting in 1962, the Lincoln Lutheran Junior High was open for students.

After forty years, six churches were a part of the association. One more elementary school joined the two elementary schools. Adding a high school to the junior high property became the mission. Tenth grade was added in 1995. Three years later, there was a big celebration for the twenty-eight students in Lincoln Lutheran's first graduating class.

Today, Messiah Lutheran (1800 South 84th Street), Faith Lutheran (8701 Adams Street) and Trinity Lutheran (1200 North 56th Street) provide education for preschool through fifth grade. At Good Shepherd Lutheran (3825 Wildbriar Lane), students can attend through eighth grade. Lincoln Lutheran Schools are known for being faith-based and family-centered.

LINCOLN CHRISTIAN (CRUSADERS)

5801 South 84th Street (1951–Present)

Prayer is this school's foundation. At first, one teacher taught thirteen students at a church. Then they were able to build a four-room school at Fifty-First and Normal. Grade offerings expanded from elementary to junior high to high school. Through faith, this school grew. Commitment was another important element. Mr. Kroeker served as principal of various levels for forty-four years. Teachers came, and many stayed, which added stability to the school.

For quite a few years, the elementary and high school were at different locations. Setting up elementary classrooms in Lincoln Berean allowed funds to be accumulated for expansion. For over twenty years, both the elementary and high school have been on the same campus. Generous support has led to further opportunities. Through its almost seventy-year history, Lincoln Christian students continue to "learn about God's world in the light of His Word."

PARKVIEW CHRISTIAN SCHOOL (PATRIOTS)

4400 North 1st Street (1980–Present)

Pastor Carl Godwin started this school for his Calvary Community congregation. Private schools were not always permissible. In 1983, a judge ordered it to close at the end of the year. With many praying on the school's behalf, it chose to stay open. The following spring, the Nebraska State Legislature passed a law permitting church and home schools to operate without a permit. Calvary is now fully accredited.

At first, classes were only offered through eighth grade. In two years, a high school was added. This smaller school allows students to be "known, challenged and loved."

Appendix 1

HISTORICAL LINCOLN RESIDENCES

Because particular places are worth protecting, they are placed on the National Historic Register or are noted as local landmarks. This is due to their architectural significance or to recognize those who called the place home. Noteworthy places with public access were mentioned throughout the book.

Even though these private residential locations are only open occasionally for tours, they are accessible by car. In case you have ever driven by and wondered about certain elaborate homes, this list is for you. The primary source for this list is the Lincoln City Planning Department Historic Preservation website. The site also includes information about certain historic Lincoln districts, as well as noteworthy fraternities and sororities.

DOWNTOWN

Koop House, 1401 South 15th Street: With great views of the capitol, George Berlinghof designed this "academic eclectic" home for a downtown retailer.

Little-Atwood House, 740 South 17th Street: Little was Lincoln Street Railway Company's president. Atwood, who purchased the house next, was a contractor and stonemason. Possibly inspired by Chicago's 1893 Columbian Exposition, this house was a longtime bed-and-breakfast.

President and Ambassador Apartments, 1330 and 1340 Lincoln Mall: These reinforced concrete apartments with brick veneer and limestone trim were constructed at the same time as the third capitol.

UNIVERSITY AREAS

Burnett House, 3256 Holdrege Street: Edgar was an Agricultural College associate dean and eventual university chancellor. Nellie was an English professor. They lived here from 1904 to at least 1938.

Hurlbut-Yates House, 720 South 16th Street: Built in 1891, this home is detailed with extensive porches. The first owner was Aenease Hurlbut, a Civil War veteran, clothier and land and hotel developer. Since business slowed, he traded places with Charles and Ruth Yates for their smaller residence. For fifty years, Charles was a commerce, banking and railroad developer. The university now uses this home for various fraternities and sororities.

Jasper and Jessie Bell House, 2212 Sheldon Street: This well-known Lincoln carpenter constructed his home.

Kiesselhach House, 3232 Holdrege Street: Known as "Mr. Corn," Theodore Kiesselhach was a university agronomist who developed corn hybrids that improved production across the state.

Lewis-Syford House, 700 North 16th Street: Presbyterian Church missionary Lewis built this house east of the university. Later, the Syfords owned the house for six decades and were gradually surrounded by Greek Row. After a period of state ownership, it is now privately owned again. This home, with its French Empire style, including a mansard roof with iron cresting, is unusual in the plains.

Terrace Houses: These are row houses turned apartments in original Lincoln. Both Barr Terrace (Eleventh and M) and Lyman Terrace (Eleventh and H) were built by notable architect Ferdinand Fisk. Baldwin Terrace (Twelfth and K); Helmer-Winnett-White Flats (Tenth–Eleventh near K).

SOUTH AND NEAR SOUTH

Amen House, 601 D Street: H.J. was a German Russian grocer who helped other immigrants by providing passage to the United States. Then he helped them transition to Lincoln life by finding housing and being their translator. This house's location next to the museum is fitting.

Betz and VanAndel Houses, Thirteenth and D Streets: Examples of the American foursquare.

Bowman-Cameron House, 1201 D Street: Both of these early owners were influential Lincoln citizens.

Bryan House, 1625 D Street: The first Lincoln house where Williams Jennings Bryan and his wife, Mary Baird Bryan, lived was initially purchased by her parents. They made the move from Illinois with them. The house has changed over time. On the former balcony, Bryan would talk to crowds that gathered to hear him speak.

Burckhardt House, 1236 Washington Street: Anna was a well-known artist and teacher. Reverend Oliver J. was assistant state penitentiary chaplain and helped start the Lincoln chapter of the NAACP.

Burgess Homestead, 6501 Southwest Fortieth Street: This foursquare farmhouse actually had six upstairs bedrooms to support the Burgesses' large family and prosperous lifestyle. Today it is a bed-and-breakfast.

Calhoun (or Skinner) House, 1130 Plum Street: This home was constructed from plans found in a magazine.

Candy House, 1003 H Street: Albert Candy was a professor of "pure mathematics" at the university for decades.

Clark House, 1937 F Street: Banker John Clark owned this Queen Anne home with many window styles. The porch and grand staircase were added later. After 1946, the house became apartments.

Everett House, 2433 Woodscrest Avenue: This 1922 Italian villa is symmetrical. At the time of construction, only two other homes were found near Lindbergh's favorite airfield. Several years later, an airplane crashed into the roof, so the owner had special roof supports added to "plane proof" the structure.

Fawell House, 2401 Ryons Street: Investment company treasurer George and his wife, Mary, owned this Mediterranean villa. In the 1920s, surgeon Artemus McKinnon and his family lived there.

Foster House, 1021 D Street: An 1881 Queen Anne–style home.

Gillen House, 2245 A Street: The front porch was oriented toward Mrs. Gillen's noteworthy gardens rather than toward the streets. Mr. Gillen operated the Haymarket Gillen & Boney candy company at Eighth and P Streets.

Grainger House, 1970 B Street: This lot once held the Mount Emerald mansion owned by the Fitzgeralds. The wife subdivided their ten acres of land to pay debts. The house burned to the ground soon after. Their basement was stockpiled with weapons to help the Irish Land League. Alice and Joseph Grainger, wholesale grocer vice president, built this house in 1910.

Hall House, 1139 D Street: Attorney Frank and his wife, Anna, longtime university supporters, moved into this ten-year-old house in 1894. Their Hall art collection became the foundation of the Sheldon Art Museum.

Heidenreich House, 1204 Peach Street: Charles was a cigar maker who lived in this 1912 house with his wife, Augusta. They sold it to Trinity Lutheran to use as a parsonage. Later, the home was Ruby & Cordelia's Fine Tea Room. Today it is a private residence.

Hitchcock House, 2733 Sheridan Boulevard: Designed in 1922 for an auto dealer's family, this residence and carriage house includes extensive historic landscaping with multiple hedges.

Lau House, 1818 South 24th Street: H.C. Lau, vice president of his family's wholesale grocery, married Margaret Honeywell. This Lincoln addition was named for her family. They lived near her brother and parents.

Maple Lodge (Ziemer House), 2030 Euclid Avenue: Arriving to Lincoln in 1870, Ziemer was a Burlington Railroad ticket agent, an interior designer and Christian Science healer. The house is covered in wooden shingles. By adding windows to the front porch, they created a winter solarium. Copper gutters carried rainwater to the underground cistern. The adjacent grounds are now a small Lincoln park.

McAfee House, 1801 C Street: This home was built in 1915 from plans purchased at the Chicago World's Fair. With multilevel balconies, the home has a solarium with an Italian ceramic tile fountain and floor.

Pauley House, 2540 C Street: At age twenty-six, Ray Pauley, an employee for his father's Pauley Lumber, built this 1918 prairie school–style home that was possibly based on Barnes book design plans.

Phillips Castle, 1845 D Street: This Richardsonian Romanesque–style stone house included forty rooms decorated in Victorian style. The fifteen fireplaces and round turret demonstrated the era's extravagance. R.O. Phillips built towns along the Burlington and Missouri River Railroad line in Nebraska, Kansas and Colorado. Involved in area politics and committees, Phillips lost his fortune in the 1890s. For more than twenty years, the Whedon family lived here. Later, this location was a fraternity house and nursing home before becoming apartments.

Reimers Bungalow, 2201 B Street: Emily Reimers of Reimers-Kauffman Concrete designed this concrete block home.

Ricketts House, #2 2125 B Street: Attorney Arnott lived here with second wife, Elizabeth. Their house was once part of the Rogers House offerings.

Roberts House, 3158 Sheridan Boulevard: This was designed by seventy-five-year-old Artemas Roberts for his son.

Rogers House, 2145 B Street: Now a bed-and-breakfast, Noyes and Harriet Rogers built this 1914 mansion. After leaving Minden Bank, Noyes directed Lincoln's Central National Bank.

Ryons-Alexander House, 1845 Ryons Street: William Ryons, son of Irishman Joseph, was longtime First National Bank vice president and built this house in 1908. The next resident was Dr. Hartley Burr Alexander, philosophy professor at the University of Nebraska, whose achievements in the fields of philosophy, architecture and anthropology were notable. He planned the third capitol's themes and inscriptions.

WOODSHIRE NEIGHBORHOOD

This neighborhood was planned by Lincolnite landscape artist, Ernst Herminghaus.

Schaaf House, 659 South 18th Street: As well as building neighborhoods, C.A. Scaaf constructed his own 1920 bungalow. Materials were partially from his millwork factory.

Sidles House, 2110 A Street: This was one of architect Fiske's significant designs. Businessman H.E. Sidles's home eventually housed multiple university chancellors.

Spalding House, 2221 Sheridan Boulevard: With fine woodwork from his lumberyard, Frank lived here with his wife, Julia. This first Woods Brothers' Sheridan Boulevard development house was started before all nearby lots were plotted.

Thayer House, 1901 Prospect Street: Governor John and First Lady Mary Thayer lived in this house purchased from architect George Peters.

Tyler House, 808 D Street: William Tyler's architect brother designed his home complete with the octagonal tower and sandstone ornamentation. This advertised that their 1881 Tyler Stone Company supplied quality stone for many notable buildings.

Watkins House, 920 D Street: Newspaper publisher Albert Watkins wrote one of Nebraska's first histories with J. Sterling Morton. Colored glass and decorated trim showcase the Queen Anne style.

Wheeler House, 1717 D Street: During his fifty years as a court reporter, Myron wrote reports by hand before getting one of Nebraska's first typewriters. As "dean of American court reporters," he used a Dictaphone in later years. His 1891 house, shared with his wife, Cora, is complex with its jagged roofline and multiple shingle patterns covering the sides.

Woods House, 2501 Sheridan Boulevard: National landscape architect Jens Jensen designed the grounds while Chicagoan Paul Hyland designed this large Italian Renaissance Revival for Frank and Nelle.

BETHANY, UNIVERSITY PLACE AND HAVELOCK

Beattie-Miles House, 6706 Colby Street: Constructed for a Cotner College professor, this is the last building associated directly with that school.

MIDTOWN
South of O

Cordner House, 325 South 55th Street: The owner/architect designed this cross-gambrel Dutch Colonial Revival. The acreage included orchards and poultry. In 1948, the land was subdivided.

Dial House, 2952 Washington Street: Elias was a rural mail carrier. His architect/builder, George Ridgeway, worked around Lincoln for thirty-six years. This combined Queen Anne and Neo-Classical Revival demonstrates that current trends impact designs.

Guy and Mary Brown Houses, 219–221 South 27th Street: This house is from Lincoln's first decade. Guy was a state librarian and Nebraska Supreme Court clerk/reporter during the state's early days.

Hac Grocery, 2943 Garfield Street: For forty years, this building was the Hac Grocery, the Hac residence and the Chimes, where their daughter offered music lessons. Today it is apartments.

Lally House, 22541 North Street: This Queen Anne–style house symbolizes Lincoln's 1880s growth. Frank Lally, university farm janitor, lived here with his daughter, Eleanor, who taught at Elliot School.

Murphy-Sheldon House, 2525 N Street: Owned by real estate agents, this property with porches and a carriage house was on Lincoln's eastern edge. Later owner Frances Sheldon's estate funded the Sheldon Museum of Art.

Park-Hill, 1913 South 41st Street: Roberts and Woods built this in 1896 for Louis Young. Dr. Faulkner, Woodmen Accident/Assurity Life founder, lived here from 1900 to 1927.

Ricketts House, #1 400 South 33rd Street: Lincoln city attorney Arnold lived in this country-style house with his first wife, Louisa. Later Woods Park took over the Rogers tract houses across the street.

Ross House, 445 South 30th Street: Nimrod, one of Lincoln's first African American policemen, lived in this 1903 home. His athletic son, Clinton, was the first African American University of Nebraska law graduate.

Stake House, 145 South 28th Street: Berlinghof designed this 1919 brick/limestone home with a green glazed roof. It was finished by local builder Stake for his family.

Weil House, 1129 South 17th Street: Morris Weil, Bank of Commerce founder, lived with his family in this Neo-Classical Revival–style house for fifty years. Later owners were a nursing home, a bed-and-breakfast and a university fraternity.

Yost House, 1900 South 25th Street: A German Russian owner of multiple lumberyards lived in this Berlinhof-designed home.

Zimmer Grocery Store and House, 1941 K Street: Jacob Zimmer and his family lived in this 1904 house and added a grocery in 1906. Various businesses used the store while the house was still a residence.

North of O

Armstrong-Davis House, 545 North 26th Street: In 1914, a doctor built this north of his medical practice. Various family members owned the house for more than seventy years. In 1985, the property changed hands. The copper caned stained-glass windows are original.

Cultura Duplex, 525 North 25th Street: The Culturas owned Rowan, Cultura & Co., a coffee, tea and spice business at Eighth and P Streets.

Eddy-Taylor House, 425 North 25th Street: In 1891, local developer Amborse Eddy constructed this and surrounding homes. In 1902, Harvard graduate William George Langworthy Taylor purchased it. This head of the university political economy department was a world traveler and expert horseman. Later, fraternities and sororities were housed here.

Kiesselbach House, 3232 Holdrege Street: Theodore Kisselbach knew corn. The hybrids he developed increased corn production and profitability.

McWilliams House, 1723 North Twenty-Ninth Street: Trago T. and Ida Belle McWilliams helped make life better for Lincoln's African

American community through business ownership, church and civil rights activism. Their son became an area pastor. Trago Park, next to the Malone Center, honors both father and son.

Reynolds House, 2530 Q Street: This American foursquare house alternated concrete block patterns. Dr. O.C. Reynolds was a prominent Lincoln physician/surgeon and president of medical staff at Saint Elizabeth Hospital.

Royers-Williams House, 407 North 26th Street: Royers built this 1880s home. In 1898, Dr. Hattie Plum Williams, university sociologist, documented Lincoln's Germans from Russian communities. She and her husband, Thomas, added the front porch.

Slattery House, 5230 North 14th Street: Part of a farmstead once far from Lincoln, this Tutor was designed by Fiske and Meginnis. Dr. Slattery was important to the local medical community.

Taylor House, 2721 P Street: This Italianate 1890 house was owned by John and Levina Taylor. His farmland east of Lincoln became Taylor Park and Taylor Meadows.

East of Fifty-Sixth Street

Griswold House, 1256 Fall Creek Road: This was built for Robert Southgate Griswold in the newer Piedmont Development. He would later take over his cousin's seed company. Their seed elevator is still at Eighth and North Streets.

Rees House, 4701 Bancroft Street: This Art Moderne home was built in 1938. Not only did Professor David represent the Seventh-day Adventist Central Conference, but he also managed the nearby Christian Record braille publishing house. His wife, Anna, was the organization's librarian.

Appendix 2

LINCOLN ARTISTS

L incoln values art. Around town, outdoor sculptures can be seen. Many buildings feature work, galleries contain pieces and some are even found at Lincoln's art museums. These are the artists to look for around town who are quite connected to Lincoln and who have contributed to the art scene.

David Monrose lived in Lincoln for his last fifty years. He did circus painting. His fourteen-foot mural at the Fourteenth and Q auto dealership was notable. His *Old Main Library* is at Bennett Martin Library.

Dwight Kirsch* directed the University of Nebraska Art Galleries at Morrill Hall from 1936 until 1950. His *Over the Housetops of Lincoln* was painted in 1934 right after the capitol construction was complete.

Elizabeth Dolan's public murals include *World Peace* at UNL Union Women's Lounge and *Three Panels of a Child's* at Bennett Martin Library.

Francisco Souto is currently the director of the School of Art, Art History and Design at the University of Nebraska–Lincoln. Born in Venezuela, his art works include still life, photography and design.

Gail Butt's* oil, encaustic and watercolor paintings feature bold colors and abstract shapes that result in realistic depictions.

James Eisentrager* painted with bold lines and considered himself a structuralist. Some of his paintings included baseball as a theme. His *Lancaster #11* is at Bennett Martin Library.

Julee Lowe created art out of glass. Around Lincoln, numerous churches display her stained glass. One interesting piece is the Saint Mark's Episcopal Church processional cross. Her first commissioned piece was completed for

Southview Christian Church. Growing up, she hoped that she could help make her childhood church prettier. Her dream came true.

Karen Kunc* is a master of the woodcut medium and works out of the Constellations art studio.

Keith Jacobshagen's* works often feature Lincoln and include both black-and-white photographs and painted landscapes.

Leonard Thiessen was Nebraska Arts Council's executive secretary from 1966 until 1974. Thiessen created paintings, murals, sculptures and more. He collaborated on the Pershing Auditorium on the 140-by-38-foot tile mural with William Hammon of Omaha.

Lynn Dance worked with Robert Starck to document Nebraska in black and white. Their efforts added to the 1977 American Centennial celebration of art.

Thomas Coleman's* style was compared to Goya, and his works were complex and often in black and white.

Born in Beatrice, **Weldon Kees** graduated from UNL. He went on to be a significant 1940s poet. Also a creator, many of his paintings feature bold colors and geometric shapes. His *Red Entrance* is at Bennett Martin Library.

IMAGES IN BRICK

Jay Tschetter sculpts out of brick. His locations include:

Cornhusker Hotel Marriott Lincoln "City of Lincoln" seal
Russ' Market Grocery Store at Seventeenth and Washington
Bison and Locomotive mural in the Iron Horse Pub at Legacy Retirement
    Communities gathering room
Pioneer Legacy Retirement Home
Former Imhoff House at Twelfth and Lincoln Mall
F Street Community Center

*Denotes this person has been a UNL art assistant or professor at one point.

HISTORICAL LINCOLN ARCHITECTS

Through the years, these three architectural firms designed multiple Lincoln buildings. Linking architects to multiple places helps connect the dots. The dates are based on completion. This is not an exhaustive list.

DAVIS DESIGN

Many Lincoln buildings can be credited to one firm. Son of a university professor, newly graduated Ellery Davis took a job as a draftsman in 1912. He then formed a partnership with architect George Berlinghof. Later, Davis and his colleagues made their mark as Davis and Wilson and then as Davis Fenton Stange Darling. Now, this century-old architectural firm is known simply as Davis Design. Most of the Lincoln buildings conceptualized by this visionary company are still standing today.

1912: Lincoln High School
  University of Nebraska College of Law (Old)
1914: The Miller & Paine Department Store
1916: Scottish Rite Temple
  Lincoln Commercial Club
  Bancroft Elementary School
1923: Memorial Stadium
1924: Temple of Congregation B'Nai Jeshuran

1925: Gold's Department Store
   Lincoln General Hospital—updated in 1965
1926: Randolph School
   Westminster Presbyterian Church
   The Coliseum
1927: Morrill Hall
   Stuart Building
1928: Kimball Bros. Building (now League of Human Dignity)
   Hussong Ford Building
1929: The Stuart Building
1935: Woodmen Insurance Building*
1936: Chet Ager Aviary
1938: Rudge Memorial Chapel at Wyuka
1940: Lincoln Urban League 2030 T Street
1941: Northeast High School
1943: Love Library
1953: Nebraska State Historical Society
1954: Woodmen Accident and Life
1956: Security Financial Life Insurance Company
1964: Dorsey Laboratories (now Novartis)
1967: Lincoln East Junior/Senior High
1968: First Plymouth Church updates, also 1993 and 2014 updates
1972: Seacrest Field at East High School
1973: Lincoln Airport
1976: Nebraska Wesleyan Knight Field House 1975
   National Bank of Commerce along with I.M. Pei 1974
   Bob Devaney Sports Center
1981: Nebraska Wesleyan Elder Memorial Speech and Theatre Center
1988: UNL Animal Sciences Center
1991: O Street Skywalk
1994: Burnham Yates Conference Center
   UNL George W. Beadle Center for Genetics and Biomaterials Research
   Carriage Park Parking Facility
1999: Huntington Elementary School
2000: Security Financial Life Insurance Company—brand new accommodations
2003: Ortner Center at Union College
2004: Tabitha Lifequest Center
   West Gate Bank Center

2005: Bryan Health West Campus (formerly Lincoln General Hospital)
  First National Bank
2007: Lincoln Composites
2010: Tabitha South Entrance Edition
2011: Premier Psychiatric Group
  Kawasaki Motors Manufacturing Corporation
2013: Farmer's Mutual Insurance
2014: Haymarket Parking Decks
  Independence Center for Bryan Health
2015: Greenhouse Innovation Center
2016: Wysong Elementary School
2017: The Resort at Firethorn
  Bryan Memorial Hospital: Numerous additions, updates and locations

*Denotes buildings that have been remodeled.

For almost one decade, Harry Meginnis made his mark on Lincoln. He partnered with F.C. Fiske from 1915 until 1924. Edward Schaumberg joined them in 1925 and then Fiske was independent. The other two men were architectural partners until 1951. Dates of the buildings show who was working together at the time of completion.

1905: Lincoln Drug Company/Apothecary (Fiske)
1907: East Lincoln Baptist Church (Fiske and Dieman)
1916: German Congregational Ebenezer Church
1918: Willard Elementary School
1919: Hartley Elementary School
1920: Prescott Elementary School
1921: Lincoln Power and Water Station
1922: Antelope Grocery
1923: Whittier Junior High
1925: Irving Middle School
1926: Blessed Sacrament Elementary
1927: Federal Trust Company Building
1932: YWCA
  Original Municipal Airport
1935: Masonic Temple
1936: Lincoln Liberty Life Insurance Building.
1938: McKelvie Building at 210 North Fourteenth

A.W. WOODS AND ROBERTS

A.W. Woods was not one of the Woods brothers, but he did design their first building. He started as a draftsman for Roberts, and then they became partners. Many of his properties are out of town, but a few are in Lincoln.

1914: Woods Bros. Haymarket Office
1920s: First German Congregational Church
1925: Saint Paul's Evangelical Church,
1926: Quinn Chapel African Methodist Episcopal Church
1927: Ebenezer Congregational
   Street John's Evangelical Lutheran Church

BIBLIOGRAPHY

Interviews with Author (June–November 2019)
and Those Who Supported Research

Ashley Hahn-May, NeighborWorks Lincoln.
Beth Oligmueller, Lincoln Marriott Cornhusker Hotel.
Bob Anderson, Hillcrest Country Club longtime member.
Bob Culver, National Roller Skating Museum volunteer
Bob McNally, Lincoln Airport Authority, and director of operations.
Bob Priddy, Missouri Net, regarding aviation.
Buck Kiechel, Kiechel Fine Art.
Captain Daniel Ripley, Lincoln Fire and Rescue.
Carol Krabill-McAdow, Ed.S, research volunteer, McKinley Presidential
    Library and Museum.
Carter Hulins, Lincoln Public Schools.
Dan Gutzman, formerly Mural Mural Graphics.
Daniel Ripley, captain, Lincoln Fire and Rescue.
Delloise Carroll, 17th Street Shops.
Diane Wilson, Lincoln's Bennett Martin Library Heritage Room curator.
Don Finney, Saint Paul United Methodist tour.
Ed Zimmer, Lincoln Historic Preservation planner.
Gary Seacrest.
Greg Joyce, Legacy Retirement Communities.
Harry Tompkin, Palace Glass Company.
Jeff Barnes, Nebraska author.

Jeff VanPelt, Lincoln Regional Center.
Jeremy Penrod, Temple Baptist Church pastor.
Jerry Shorney, Lincoln Parks and Recreation, retired.
Jim McKee, Lincoln historian.
Joel Green, Robber's Cave expert tour guide.
John Chapo, Lincoln Children's Zoo.
John Fabiun, Lawrence Terry Stevens Trust director.
Joshua Genrich, Saint Paul United Methodist Church historian.
Joy Citta, retired Lincoln Police captain.
Judy Batterman and Pastor Dan Warnes, First Lutheran Church.
Judy Schrader, Saint Patrick's Church in Havelock longtime member.
Kathie Johnson and Krista Rickman, First Plymouth Congregational Church.
Kathleen Dering, Elliott Elementary School principal.
Kat Scholl, Lincoln Parks and Recreation.
Kay Logan-Peters, University of Nebraska.
Lance Todd, Larsen Tractor Test and Power Museum.
Leona Frerichs, forty-three-plus-year secretary, Havelock United Methodist
    Church.
Leta Powell-Drake, broadcaster extraordinaire.
Lorraine Moon, Nebraska Center for Energy Sciences Research.
Marco Pedroza, Scott Middle School principal.
Marj Rohlfs and Betty Petersen, former Lincoln Christian teachers.
Martha Brown, Lincoln Visitors Center.
Martha Sorensen, First Baptist Church historian.
MaryBeth McWilliams, Bryan Health volunteer coordinator.
Matt Metcalf, Davis Design.
Michelle deRusha, Lincoln author.
Mike DeKalb, White Hall Mansion.
Nanci Gasiel, Salvation Army Central USA museum director.
Nancy Coren, Congregation Tiffereth Israel lay leader.
Oliver Pollak, Nebraska Carnegie Libraries expert.
Pat Anderson, NeighborWorks.
Peter Mullin, South Street Temple.
Rachel Johnson, Lincoln Regional Center.
Randi Zabel, Lincoln Housing Authority (Air Park area expert).
Retired colonel Gerald Meyer, Nebraska National Guard Museum.
Rhonda Cann, National Roller Skating Museum.
Robb Rexilius, First Street Bible Church.
Robert Scott, WRK.

Rod Scott, Architectural Glassarts.

Roxanne Smith, Office of Nebraska Capitol Commission tourism supervisor.

Ryan Teller, Integrated Marketing and Communications Union College executive director.

Safairra Hutchinson, Rococco Theatre/Stuart Building.

Scott Shafer, Nebraska Commission of Indian Affairs.

Sherry Pawelko, retired executive director of the American Historical Society of Germans from Russia.

Sid Conner, Conner's Architectural Antiques.

Sister Patricia Radik M.S., Catholic Diocese of Lincoln archivist.

Stephanie Grace Whitson, Nebraska author.

Stephanie Wolf, Whitehall Mansion.

Steve Nosal, Sunken Gardens/Hamann Rose Garden supervisor.

Tom J. Frye, author and Havelock expert.

Tom McKitterick, Country Club of Lincoln.

Books

Barnes, Jeff *150@150: Nebraska's Landmark Buildings at the State's Sesquicentennial.* Brookfied, MO: Donning Company, 2017.

Berry, Harold J. *I Love to Tell the Story*. Lincoln, NE: Good News Broadcasting, 1989.

Booth, Ethel. *Where Sunflowers Grew: The Story of Nebraska Wesleyan through Its Early Years.* Lincoln: NE, Wesleyan Press, 1962.

Boye, Alan. *The Complete Roadside Guide to Nebraska.* Street Johnsbury, VT: Saltillo Press, 1989.

Brown, Elinor L. *Architectural Wonder of the World*. Ceresco, NE: Midwest Publishing Company, 1965.

———. *Discovery and History of the Hudson Log Cabin.* Ceresco, NE: Midwest Publishing, 2005.

———. *History of Lancaster County, Then and Now.* N.p., 1971.

Bryan, William Jennings, and Mary Baird Bryan. *The Memoirs of William Jennings Bryan.* Chicago: John C. Winston Company, 1925.

Burchfield, Gary. *Seasons of Lincoln.* Montgomery, AL: Community Communication, 2001.

Clark and Enersen, Hamersky, Schlaebitz, Burroughs and Thomsen. *Wilderness Park, Lancaster County, Nebraska: A Master Plan for Its Use and Management Prepared for Lincoln.* Lincoln, NE: n.p., 1972.

Colburn, Faith A. *From Picas to Bytes: Four Generations of Seacrest Newspaper Service to Nebraska*. Self-published, Create Space, 2014.

Collins, Molly S. *Local and Oral History in Lincoln, Nebraska: A Bibliography*. Lincoln: Nebraska Committee for the Humanities, 1983.

Dick, Everett. *The Sod-House Frontier, 1854–1890*. New York: Appleton-Century Co., 1954. First published 1937.

———. *Union College of the Golden Cords*. Lincoln, NE: Union College Press, 1967.

Dick, Everett, and David D. Rees. *Union College: Fifty Years of Service*. Lincoln, NE: Union College Press, 1941.

Dick, Everett, George Gibson and Union College Staff. *Union College: Light Upon the Hill*. Lincoln, NE: Union College, 2004.

Duling, Van C., and Jerry Mapes. *Lincoln Scrapbook*. Lincoln, NE: J and L Lee Co., 2003.

Federal Writers' Project of the Works Progress Administration State of Nebraska. *Lincoln City Guide*. Lincoln, NE: Woodruff Printing Co., 1937.

Frolik, Elvin F., and Ralston J. Graham. *College of Agriculture of the University of Nebraska–Lincoln: The First Century*. Lincoln, NE: Board of Regents of the University of Nebraska, 1987.

Gartner, Ruth E. *The Lincoln High Story, 1871–1971*. Lincoln, NE: Arbor Printing Company, 1971.

Geske, Norman A. *Art and Artists in Nebraska*. Lincoln: University of Nebraska–Lincoln, Sheldon Memorial Art Gallery, 1983.

Goerres, Vince. *Wings Over Nebraska: Historic Aviation Photographs*. Lincoln: Nebraska State Historical Society, 2010.

Gosen, Sister Loretta. *History of the Catholic Church in the Diocese of Lincoln, Nebraska 1887–1987*. Lincoln, NE: Catholic Bishop of Lincoln, 1986.

Green, Joel. *Robber's Cave: Truths, Legends, Recollections*. Lincoln, NE: Mighty Son's Publications, 2018.

Hartman, Douglas R. *Nebraska's Militia: The History of the Army and Air National Guard, 1854–1991*. Virginia Beach, VA: Donning Company/Publishers, 1994.

Hickey, Donald R. *Nebraska Moments: Glimpses of Nebraska's Past*. Lincoln: University of Nebraska Press, 1992.

Hildegard Center for the Arts. *Seeking the Light*. Lincoln, NE: Jacob North Companies, 2011.

Hillegass, Linda. *City Shapers: Five Events that Defined Lincoln*. Lincoln, NE: Lincoln Lancaster Star Venture, 1987.

Hotzclaw, Jean D., and Henry F. *First Presbyterian Church, 1869–1994: A History*. Lincoln, NE: Joe Christensen Inc., 1994.

————. *A History of the First Presbyterian Church of Lincoln, Nebraska: The First One Hundred and Twenty-Five Years 1869–1994*. Lincoln, NE: First Presbyterian Church of Lincoln, 1994.

Junior League of Lincoln, Nebraska. *An Architectural Album*, Lincoln, NE: Jacob North Printing Company, 1979.

Kiple, David L. *The Street Francis Chapel Windows: Glory in Glass*. Lincoln, NE: n.p., 1998.

Korbelik, Jeff. *Lost Restaurants of Lincoln Nebraska*. Charleston, SC: The History Press, 2018.

Lancaster County Sherriff's Office. *The Sesquicentennial History of the Lancaster County Sheriff's Office, 1861–2011*. Omaha, NE: T. Print Inc., 2011.

Lincoln, Nebraska's Capital City, 1867-1923. Lincoln, NE: Woodruff Printing Company, 1923.

Lincoln Commercial Club. *Lincoln: Its Suburbs and Pleasure Resorts*. Lincoln, NE: N.p., 1913.

Lincoln Haymarket Development Corporation. *Historic Haymarket*. Lincoln, NE: N.p., 2014.

Lindbergh, Charles A. *Autobiography of Values*. New York: Harcourt Brace Jovanovich, 1976.

Ling, Bettina. *Willa Cather: Author and Critic*. New York: Franklin Watts, 2003.

Logan-Peters, Kay. *University of Nebraska–Lincoln*. Charleston, SC: Arcadia Publishing, 2017.

Luebke, Frederick C. *Harmony of the Arts: The Nebraska State Capitol*. Lincoln: University of Nebraska Press, 1990.

Manley, Robert N. *Centennial History of the University of Nebraska: I Frontier University, 1869–1919*. Lincoln: University of Nebraska Press, 1969.

Manton, Charlotte. *The Community of Lincoln, Nebraska*. Lincoln, NE: Lincoln Public Schools, 1997.

Masters, Margaret Dale. *Hartley Burr Alexander: Writer-in-Stone*. Lincoln, NE: Jacob North Printing Company, 1992.

McArthur, Jeff. *The Great Heist*. Burbank, CA: Bandwagon Books, 2013.

McKee, James L. *Lincoln: The Prairie Capital, An Illustrated History*. Lincoln, NE: J and L Lee Co., n.d.

————. *Remember When: Memories of Lincoln*. Lincoln, NE: J and L Lee Co., 1998.

————. *Visions of Lincoln: Nebraska's Capital City in the Present, Past and Future*. N.p.: Tank Works, LLC, 2007.

McKee, James L., and Arthur Duerschener. *Lincoln: A Photographic History*. Lincoln, NE: Salt Valley Press, 1976.

McKee, James L., Edward F. Zimmer and Lori K. Jorgensen. *Havelock: A Photo History and Walking Tour.* Lincoln, NE: J and L Lee Co., 1993.

McKelvie, Martha Groves. *Presidents, Politicians & People I Have Known.* Philadelphia, PA: Franklin Publishing Company, 1970.

Meltzer, Milton. *Willa Cather: A Biography.* Minneapolis, MN: Twenty-First Century Books, 2008.

Miller and Paine. *The Prairie Capital.* Lincoln, NE: Miller and Paine, 1930.

Nebraska High School Historical Society. *Pages of History: Nebraska High Schools: Present and Past-Public and Private, 1854–1994.* Lincoln: Nebraska High School Historical Society, 1994.

Nebraska University College of Architecture. *Historic & Architectural Site Survey.* Lincoln: University of Nebraska, 1978.

Nelson, O.M. *Swedes in Lincoln and Vicinity.* Lincoln, NE: O.M. Nelson, 1936.

Nielsen, Mary Jane. *Life in Lincoln as We Remember It.* Lincoln, NE: MJN Vision LLC, 2007.

———. *A Street Named "O."* Lincoln, NE: MJN Vision LLC, 2007.

———. *The Year 2000 & Beyond: Lincoln Women Leading the Way.* Lincoln, NE: Dageforde Publishing, 1999.

Nielsen, Mary Jane, and Jonathan Roth. *Lincoln Looks Back.* Lincoln: Nebraska Printing Center, 2009.

———. *When I Was a Kid.* Lincoln, NE: JMJ Inspirations LLC, 2009.

Nielsen, Mary Jane, Jonathan Roth, Beth Vogel and Russ Vogel. *Game Day Memories: Tailgaters, Touchdowns & Traditions.* Lincoln, NE: Settell's Printing, 2010.

Perkey, Elton A. *Perkey's Nebraska Place Names.* 4th ed. Lincoln, NE: J and L Lee Co., 2003.

Pickard, George. *Titans and Heroes of American Roller Skating.* Lincoln, NE: National Museum of Roller Skating, 2010.

Pollak, Oliver B. *Jewish Life in Omaha and Lincoln: A Photographic History.* Charleston, SC: Arcadia Publishing, 2001.

———. *A State of Readers: Nebraska's Carnegie Libraries.* Lincoln, NE: Lee's Booksellers, 2005.

Railway Publishing Company. *The Capital City, Lincoln, Nebraska: The Educational Capital of the Middle West.* Lincoln, NE: N.p., 1901.

Riley, James Whitcomb. *The Complete Poetical Works of James Whitcomb Riley.* New York: Grosset and Dunlap, 1973.

Saint Patrick's Parish. *Faith and Hard Work: A Story of Saint Patrick's Parish of Lincoln, Nebraska.* N.p., 1993.

Sawyer, R. McLaran. *Centennial History of the University of Nebraska: II Frontier University, 1920–1969.* Lincoln: University of Nebraska Press, 1969.

Seymour, Margaret R. *The Unitarian Church of Lincoln, Nebraska, The First Hundred Years 1898–1998.* N.p., 1998.

Sheldon, A.E. *Nebraska Old and New.* Lincoln, NE: University Publishing Company, 1937.

Sheldon Memorial Art Gallery. *A Selection of Works from the Art Collections at the University of Nebraska.* Lincoln, NE: N.p., 1963.

Stanton, Frank. *Dedication of the Sheldon Memorial Art Gallery.* Lincoln, NE: Sheldon Memorial Art Gallery, 1963.

Starita, Joe, and Tom Tidball. *A Day in the Life of the Fans of Memorial Stadium.* Lincoln: Nebraska Book Publishing Company, 1996.

Swartzlander, David, Ed. *Unforgettable: The Photos of Our Lives.* Lincoln, NE: Lincoln Journal Star, 2001.

Welsch, Roger L. *Inside Lincoln (The Things They Never Tell You!).* Lincoln, NE: Plains Heritage, 1984.

White, Debra Kleve. *The Spirit of Nebraska: A History of Husker Game Day Traditions the Tunnel Walk, Mascots, Cheer & More.* Lincoln, NE: Cheerful Books, 2019.

Williams, Hattie Plum. *The Czar's Germans: With Particular Reference to the Volga Germans.* Lincoln, NE: American Historical Society of Germans from Russia, 1975.

Zimmer, Ed. *Wyuka Cemetery: A Driving & Walking Tour.* Lincoln, NE: Wyuka Historical Foundation, 2009.

Thesis Papers

Dickinson, Loren. "Public Address, Theatre and Interpretation at the Epworth League Assembly in Lincoln, Nebraska." University of Lincoln–Nebraska, 1960.

Donahue, Neoma Moffitt. "Public Parks in the Recreation Movement in Nebraska with Special Reference to Lincoln 1890–1935." University of Lincoln–Nebraska, 1935.

Johnson, Anne C. "Historic Landscape Preservation: A Case Study of Pioneers Park in Lincoln, Nebraska." University of Lincoln–Nebraska, 1993.

Robertson, Catherine S. "The Development of a Commercial Landscape in Lincoln, Nebraska, 1880–1920." University of Lincoln–Nebraska, 1983.

Sawyers, Keith. "Five Volga-German-American Houses. South Bottoms Historic District." University of Lincoln–Nebraska, 1986.

Williams, Hattie Plum. "A Social Study of the Russian German." University of Lincoln–Nebraska, 1916.

Miscellaneous

An Architectural Tour of UNL. historicbuildings.unl.edu.

Constellation Studios. https://constellation-studios.net.

Cornhusker Hotel Resources, including a Lincoln Guide from the 1980s and numerous in-house promotional materials.

Dahl, Sam. "First Lutheran Church: A Century of Life and Growth: 1870–1970." Centennial Sunday bulletin.

"Faith and Hard Work." A Story of Saint Patrick's Parish Lincoln, Nebraska.

Genrich, Joshua. "Thematic History of Saint Paul United Methodist Church." Powerpoint.

Haymarket Landmark District Walking Tour.

Historic Architectural Site Survey of South Salt Creek Lincoln, NEBR.

Jacobs, Leland. "The Cold War Comes to Lincoln: The Lincoln Air Force Base, 1952–1966." Submitted to John A. Adams Center for Military History and Strategic Analysis Cold War Essay Contest, June 2009.

Lancaster County. "Long Range Planning." City of Lincoln Planning Department. https://lincoln.ne.gov.

Lincoln Airport Authority. *Journey Through the First Fifty Years of the Lincoln Airport.* 2010.

Lincoln Country Club. *One Hundred Year Anniversary.* 2003.

Lincoln Housing Authority. "Air Park Subdivisions Information."

———. "Lincoln Army Airfield Regimental Chapel."

Lincoln Journal-Star.

Lincoln Kids! Newspaper.

Lincoln Sunday Star. August 2, 1914.

Lincoln Visitor's Center Docent Files.

McKee, Jim, Dr. James Hewitt, James VanNurden, Sharon Kennedy, Captain Joy Citta, Rob Brauning and Ed Zimmer. History Nebraska Brown Bag Lecture Series, 2011–19.

The Nebraska Capitol. Lincoln: Nebraska State Capitol Commission, 1926.

Nebraska Department of Education. https://www.education.ne.gov.

Nebraska Hall of Fame. Lincoln, NE: Cosponsored by the Nebraska Hall of Fame Commission and the Nebraska Association for the Education of Young Children website.

NEBRASKALand Foundation, Inc, 1997.

Nebraska State Historical Society. Place Makers of Nebraska: The Architects." http://www.e-nebraskahistory.org.

Nebraska State Journal.

Nebraska Wesleyan University. "Past Presidents." President's Office. https://www.nebrwesleyan.edu.

140th Year Committee. *First Christian Church 1869–2009.*

Poetry Foundation. "James Whitcomb Riley." https://www.poetryfoundation.org.

Prairie Creek Inn Bed-and-Breakfast Brochure on the Leavitt House.

Rife, Janet. *First Baptist Church 150th Anniversary.*

Saint Paul United Methodist Church Ninetieth Anniversary History brochure. 1947.

Salvation Army Lincoln Chapter.

Sheffield, Wesley. "The Community Mental Health Act of 1963: Still Pursuing the Promise of Reform Fifty Years Later." Young Minds Advocacy. https://www.ymadvocacy.org.

Sunday Journal-Star. Lincoln's 1966 Citizens' Report Supplement. April 2, 1967.

Wells Fargo. "A Renowned Architect's Influence in Lincoln, Nebraska." Wells Fargo Stories. https://stories.wf.com.

Williams, F.A. "First Christian Church 75th Anniversary Meeting." January 28, 1944.

For additional consulted sources, refer to OdysseyThroughNebraska.com. Articles from newspapers.com are available upon request.

INDEX

ABOUT THE AUTHOR

Native Nebraskan Gretchen Garrison loves to explore the stories that define her state. Understanding more about Nebraska places and people—both past and present—has become her mission. She considers it a privilege that she gets to tell these tales through her articles, books and speaking engagements.

Gretchen and her husband, Kyle, are raising their four kids on a southeast Nebraska acreage property where God paints the best sunrises. Her first The History Press book, *Detour Nebraska: Historical Destinations and Natural Wonders*, was published in 2017.